Building Recovery Resilience

The first workbook written for individuals progressing through the Recovery Resilience Program, a person-centered, strength and resiliency-based relapse prevention and recovery-oriented intervention designed for individuals in addiction recovery. The book presents practices derived from the I-System Model and the evidence-based intervention Mind-Body Bridging that enhance "recovery resilience" – a term we use to refer to an individual's capacity to effectively apply coping and self-regulation skills in dealing with cravings, triggers, stress, and high-risk situations without reverting to substance use. Each chapter introduces various Recovery Resilience Practices and explains how they can positively augment any recovery pathway. Readers can learn to use these practices through various exercises, which they can complete before moving on to the next chapter. The program helps individuals to draw upon and use their recovery capital (for example, skills, tools, knowledge, etc.), remove barriers along the way, and strengthen their internal resources, and ultimately reach recovery and life goals.

Guy du Plessis is a researcher and instructor at the I-System Institute for Transdisciplinary Studies at Utah State University and a faculty member at the Institute for Advanced Psychotherapy at Loyola University Chicago. He studied psychology and philosophy at the University of Cape Town and University of South Africa and has worked in the mental health field for over 25 years as a counselor, clinical and program director, and has designed and managed several inpatient addiction treatment programs. He is the author and co-author of six books.

Derrik R. Tollefson is the Mind-Body Bridging Professor of Social Work and director of the I-System Institute for Transdisciplinary Studies at Utah State University. He holds a PhD in social work from the University of Utah and is a licensed clinical social worker in Utah.

Robert Weathers is an addiction educator and certified recovery coach and holds a PhD in clinical psychology. Over the course of his career, he has provided thousands of hours of therapeutic counseling to clients and has committed nearly 50 years to training graduate-level clinicians at several Southern California universities.

Kevin G. Webb is a licensed clinical social worker and an assistant professional practice professor and associate director of the I-System Institute for Transdisciplinary Studies at Utah State University.

Building Recovery Resilience

Addiction Recovery and Relapse Prevention Workbook – An I-System Model Application

Guy du Plessis

Utah State University

Derrik R. Tollefson

Utah State University

Robert Weathers

Addiction Recovery Coach, California

Kevin G. Webb

Utah State University

CAMBRIDGE
UNIVERSITY PRESS

Shaftesbury Road, Cambridge CB2 8EA, United Kingdom

One Liberty Plaza, 20th Floor, New York, NY 10006, USA

477 Williamstown Road, Port Melbourne, VIC 3207, Australia

314–321, 3rd Floor, Plot 3, Splendor Forum, Jasola District Centre, New Delhi – 110025, India

103 Penang Road, #05–06/07, Visioncrest Commercial, Singapore 238467

Cambridge University Press is part of Cambridge University Press & Assessment, a department of the University of Cambridge.

We share the University's mission to contribute to society through the pursuit of education, learning and research at the highest international levels of excellence.

www.cambridge.org
Information on this title: www.cambridge.org/9781009378819

DOI: 10.1017/9781009378772

First published 2024

Printed in the United Kingdom by CPI Group Ltd, Croydon CR0 4YY

A catalogue record for this publication is available from the British Library

Library of Congress Cataloging-in-Publication Data
Names: Du Plessis, Guy, author.
Title: Building recovery resilience : addiction recovery and relapse prevention workbook – an I-system model / Guy du Plessis, Utah State University, Derrik R. Tollefson, Utah State University, Robert Weathers, Addictions Recoversy Coach, California, Kevin G. Webb, Utah State University
Description: Cambridge, United Kingdom ; New York, NY: Cambridge University Press, 2024. | Includes bibliographical references.
Identifiers: LCCN 2023045412 | ISBN 9781009378819 (paperback) | ISBN 9781009378772 (ebook)
Subjects: LCSH: Addicts – Rehabilitation. | Recovering addicts. | Substance abuse – Treatment. | Mind and body therapies.
Classification: LCC HV4998 .D82 2024 | DDC 362.29–dc23/eng/20240112
LC record available at https://lccn.loc.gov/2023045412

ISBN 978-1-009-37881-9 Paperback

Every effort has been made in preparing this book to provide accurate and up-to-date information that is in accord with accepted standards and practice at the time of publication. Although case histories are drawn from actual cases, every effort has been made to disguise the identities of the individuals involved. Nevertheless, the authors, editors, and publishers can make no warranties that the information contained herein is totally free from error, not least because clinical standards are constantly changing through research and regulation. The authors, editors, and publishers therefore disclaim all liability for direct or consequential damages resulting from the use of material contained in this book. Readers are strongly advised to pay careful attention to information provided by the manufacturer of any drugs or equipment that they plan to use.

Contents

Contents

Introduction

"Why can't you just say, 'No'?", "Why do you have to drink so much?", and "If you really love me, you'd stop!" These and other similar questions or accusations are common course in the lives of those struggling with substance use disorders. Yet there are in fact several understandable, if perhaps counterintuitive, reasons why individuals continue to use psychoactive substances, even when the costs are so obviously high across their lives (Ahmed & Pickards, 2019; Gire, 2002; Maté, 2011; West, 2005; West, Christmas, Hastings, & Michie, 2019a).

Research points out that one reason that many individuals fail to achieve and/or maintain sobriety is that they have inadequate coping skills for dealing with stressful situations and painful feelings (Marlatt & Gordon, 1980; Miller et al., 1996). Hence, they turn to psychoactive substances as an alternative coping mechanism since alcohol or other drugs provide immediate and quite effective short-term stress relief and comfort. Some researchers believe that the primary reason psychoactive substances are so addictive is because of their capacity for providing stress reduction and emotion regulation (Brewer et al., 1998). For individuals suffering from addiction, substance use often becomes their predominant response for coping with life's challenges (Litt et al., 2003; Maté, 2011).

For those in an addiction recovery process, relapse, despite the best of intentions and efforts to stop, is a daunting challenge in any sustained and successful effort to escape addiction (Brewer et al., 1998; Marlatt, 1985a). Individuals working on profound behavior change, like recovery from addiction, are confronted again and again with powerful cravings and compulsive thoughts regarding the maladaptive behaviors they are attempting to change (Brewer, 2017). Research has revealed a direct correlation between relapse to substance use after rehabilitation and deficits in skills for coping effectively with high-risk and stressful situations (Brewer et al., 1998; Connors et al., 1993; Irvin et al., 1999). Therefore, the key to preventing relapse is to gain and practice new skills for coping with both anticipated and potentially unforeseen challenges. Simply put, having reliably accessible and effective coping skills is a crucial predictor for successful and sustained recovery from substance use disorders (Marlatt, 1985b, 1988). For this very important reason, relapse prevention books or programs typically focus on teaching such skills.

Yet, simply acquiring these coping skills does not guarantee sustained recovery. This is evidenced by the fact that addiction treatment and relapse prevention programs have high rates of relapse, despite individuals having a plethora of skills available to them and often being highly motivated for recovery (Xie et al., 2005). What we will demonstrate in *Building Recovery Resilience* is that there is often a mind-body system that hinders individuals in recovery from effectively applying these skills and recovery practices and causes them to veer off their chosen recovery pathways (Block et al., 2016; Du Plessis et al., 2021; Ho & Nakamura, 2017). The approach outlined in this workbook will teach the reader how to recognize and "befriend" this hindrance – so that instead of it being an impediment, it can assist them to stay true to their chosen recovery pathways.

Our Approach

This workbook presents practices derived from the I-System Model and the psychological intervention Mind-Body Bridging which was developed by psychoanalyst, psychiatrist, and physicist Stanley H. Block and his wife and collaborator, Carolyn Block (Block & Block, 2007; Block et al., 2020). Mind-Body Bridging,[1] has successfully been used in the treatment of several mood and behavioral disorders,[2] and has been recognized as evidence-based for the treatment of substance use disorders (Block & Du Plessis, 2018; Block et al., 2016; Nakamura et al., 2015).[3]

Three central premises inform the approach presented in this workbook. The first premise, informed by the I-System Model, is that we possess an innate capacity for resilience, self-actualization and flourishing. Patricia Giannotti and Jack Danielian in their book, *Uncovering the Resilient Core*, state that, "[f]rom the very beginning of life, the mind (like the body) is in a continuing process of working to actualize itself. The process is inherent" (Danielian & Gianotti, 2017, p. 3). Yet, the I-System Model highlights that there is a mind-body system that can obstruct and hinder our innate resilience and our natural capacity for self-actualization.[i, 4] The practices outlined in this workbook have a primary focus of teaching the reader how to identify and manage this hindrance as it manifests in their activities of daily living. Clinical experience highlights that by identifying and managing this hindrance, which we refer to as "befriending" it, we can access our natural resilience (Nakamura et al., 2015). This allows one to efficiently apply coping skills and effectively work a recovery program. Our activities of daily living become the *dojo* (the Japanese term for practice hall) for applying these practices, which help unleash our innate resilience and capacity for self-actualization and flourishing, and thus sustain us in reaching our recovery and life goals.

The second premise that informs our approach is how we define addiction,[ii] and how this relates to recovery. There is no agreed upon definition of addiction, but most addiction specialists and researchers agree on some key elements (American Psychiatric Association, 2013; Du Plessis, 2023; West, 2005; West et al., 2019a; West, Marsden & Hastings, 2019b). Our definition is

---

i We use the term "flourishing" as an umbrella term for "happiness," "well-being," and "quality of life," as we believe this is one of the best constructs to define one of the central aims of the Recovery Resilience Program, and why we have included the Flourishing Scale at the end of each chapter.

ii For the purpose of this workbook we use the terms "addiction" and "substance use disorder" interchangeably. Although the techniques in this book can be applied to both substance use and behavioral addictions, the focus of the book is on the treatment of substance use disorders. In fact, we have found the use of the term "addiction" as sometimes preferable in work with our clients in recovery, insofar as the term derives from the Latin root, *addictus*, which means "bond servant" or "slave." Hence, addiction might be understood as "servitude" or "enslavement," the alternative to which is "liberation" or "freedom" – firsthand experiences with which virtually any individual addicted to substances might readily identify.

congruent with conventional wisdom, research, and experience, but stresses one important feature that has particular relevance to the practices outlined in this workbook. We define addiction broadly and simply as a *disposition* to use psychoactive substances that is characterized by impaired control and harm. Thus, the definition of addiction we apply in this workbook views it from a dispositional perspective (proneness or tendency) that is context-dependent. Robert West and colleagues (West et al., 2019a, p. 168) define "disposition" in the context of cravings as "a latent characteristic that becomes expressed under certain conditions." This dispositional perspective highlights that individuals can vary in degrees of control depending on the context of the situation.[5] Accordingly, our approach incorporates a resiliency and strength-based approach and highlights that individuals in recovery can have the capacity to influence this disposition either by having awareness of factors that can make this disposition more likely or by having access to resources and practices that can make this disposition less likely.

The third premise, simply put, is that you cannot fix what is not broken. That is, we do not view people who experience addiction as broken. Best-selling author and recovery expert John Bradshaw presents the argument in his book *Healing the Shame that Binds You* that toxic shame is often the motivator behind addictive behaviors (as well as many other dysfunctional behaviors). He states that "[t]oxic shame gives you a sense of worthlessness, a sense of failing and falling short as a human being. Toxic shame is a rupture of the self with the self" (Bradshaw, 2005, p. 29). Toxic shame is a deep-seated belief that one is fundamentally flawed and simply not good enough as a human being. Shame often fuels substance use in a futile effort to medicate the overwhelming feelings associated with shame. Because individuals in recovery often feel flawed, not good enough, or damaged, they may feel that they need to be "fixed." Some of you reading this book might have thought this for so long that you think that it is true, that this shame is "just who I am," which may drive you to continually try and fix yourself. But these efforts are futile because we cannot fix an *illusion* or *fiction*.

The Greek myth of Sisyphus might be a useful analogy here. Sisyphus is depicted as one whose tricks and cunning as well as his hubris condemned him to eternally push a boulder uphill. However, as soon as he reached the top of the hill, the boulder would roll down and Sisyphus had to push it back up again, eternally. In trying to fix ourselves, we, like Sisyphus, keep pushing the boulder up the hill, only for it to roll down again. No matter how we try, we are caught in a perpetual cycle of trying to fix the illusory damage induced by a shame-based belief system. All types of addiction could be seen as one of being caught, like Sisyphus, in a futile and perpetual cycle. This workbook will help you to stop trying to "fix what ain't broke," and guide you in liberating yourself from that shame-based cycle. The approach outlined in this workbook does not aim to fix you, because, as you will see, there indeed is nothing to fix.

The Aim of the Workbook

This workbook outlines the **Recovery Resilience Program**, a person-centered, strength and resiliency-based relapse prevention and recovery-oriented intervention designed for individuals in addiction recovery. It will assist you in developing a **Recovery Resilience Practice** that will facilitate your addiction recovery process by enhancing your capacity to effectively work a recovery and relapse prevention program.[6] The practices presented in this workbook enhance **"recovery resilience"** – a term we use to refer to an individual's capacity to effectively apply coping and self-regulation skills in dealing with cravings, triggers, stress, and high-risk situations without reverting to substance use.

The concept of recovery resilience has commonality with the notion of *recovery capital*, a phrase used in recovery communities to refer to the sum of all internal and external resources that a person has available to initiate and maintain their ongoing recovery process (Cloud & Granfield, 2004). William White defines recovery capital as "conceptually linked to natural recovery, solution-focused therapy, strengths-based case management, recovery management, resilience and protective factors, and the ideas of hardiness, wellness, and global health" (White & Cloud, 2008, p. 23). The notion of recovery capital reflects a move away from a focus on pathology or brokenness to one of a resilience-based recovery approach – which is congruent with the Recovery Resilience Program presented in this workbook. White defines three types of recovery capital: personal recovery capital – which includes an individual's physical and human capital; family/social recovery capital – these resources relate to intimate relationships with friends and family, relationships with people in recovery, and supportive partners; and cultural capital – these resources resonate with an individual's cultural and faith-based beliefs (Foote et al., 2014; White & Cloud, 2008).

Although the Recovery Resilience Program acknowledges the importance and value of all three types of recovery capital, the primary focus is on strengthening personal recovery capital.[7] Recovery resilience specifically re-lates to the internal resources of the individual, and the aim of a Recovery Resilience Practice is to strengthen your internal resources, by removing what hinders your capacity to draw upon or use other facets of your recovery capital (e.g., skills, tools, knowledge), which will help prevent relapse, pro-mote flourishing[8] and enable you to live the good life.[9]

The Recovery Resilience Program outlined has one simple aim – to help you stay true to your recovery pathway and to help you reach your recovery and life goals, thus enabling you to flourish. Although there is a hindrance that can steer you off course, we will teach you how to "befriend" it, which will allow you to course-correct moment to moment as you go about your activ-ities of daily living. In this way, the hindrance becomes a compass that helps you stay on your recovery pathway.

How to Use This Workbook

This workbook is designed to be an adjunct to relapse prevention programs and the recovery practices of individuals in addiction recovery.[iii] The Recovery Resilience Program is ideally suited for individuals who have un-dergone initial inpatient or intensive outpatient treatment and continue to be motivated for sustained recovery.[10] Additionally, it may also be useful for individuals following a harm reduction approach, as a Recovery Resilience Practice is about "progress not perfection"[11] and therefore can serve as an adjunct to harm reduction programs.[12]

---

iii The authors would like to acknowledge and express their gratitude to Dr. Stanley Block and Carolyn Block, the developers of the I-System Model and Mind-Body Bridging, for their input in the writing and conceptualization of this workbook.

The Recovery Resilience Practice you will develop by completing this workbook is not meant to replace any of your existing recovery practices, but instead is designed to positively augment your unique recovery pathway and help you access and optimally use your recovery capital. A Recovery Resilience Practice is compatible with most recovery pathways, as well as harm reduction approaches. And its compatibility with Twelve-Step programs is emphasized because in addition to us being advocates of Twelve-Step programs, many readers of this workbook will already be engaged in a Twelve-Step fellowship and/or be participating in a Twelve-Step-oriented treatment program. Thus, a Recovery Resilience Practice is designed to support and enhance these programs. We strongly recommend that you participate in a community-based support group like the Twelve-Step program or a similar peer support group.

The workbook outlines a structured approach to progressing through the Recovery Resilience Program that can be completed within a concentrated time frame – we recommend a minimum of four to eight weeks. Each chapter in the workbook serves as a building block for the next, introducing a sequence of exercises that teach, through direct experience, aspects of a Recovery Resilience Practice as well as providing the underlying rationale for each of these practices. For all the exercises in the workbook, we will provide examples that serve as a guide for completing the exercises. We have included two scales at the end of each chapter to help you to monitor your Recovery Resilience Practice development and improvement in your subjective well-being or flourishing (Diener et al., 2010).[13]

We recommend you directly experience and live the practices introduced in each part for at least one to two weeks before moving onto the next chapter. As jazz saxophonist Charlie Parker observed: "If you don't live it, it won't come out of your horn." Which is to say: your Recovery Resilience Practice and your recovery will be sustainable only if you "live it."

1

• • • • • • • • • •

Dealing Effectively with High-Risk Situations

Every man takes the limits of his own field of vision for the limits of the world.

Arthur Schopenhauer, *"Psychological Observations,"*
Studies in Pessimism

As we pointed out in the Introduction, research has shown that having reliably accessible coping and self-regulation skills is a crucial predictor for successful, sustained recovery from addiction (Cummings et al., 1980; Marlatt, 1985b; West, 2005). With more effective skills, a person in addiction recovery develops increased confidence (Marlatt et al., 1995) in their ability to handle challenging situations without the use of substances, thereby increasing their **recovery resilience**. As mentioned, your recovery resilience represents your ability to draw on your recovery capital to effectively cope with and manage stressful situations without reverting to substance use, as well as being able to self-regulate your inner world without the use of substances.[1] Recovery resilience is about us having the right skills and the capacity to apply those skills. This is particularly important for situations that pose a high risk for relapse.

High-risk situations can be understood as events and situations that, if not effectively managed, pose a potential risk for relapse (Brewer et al., 1998).

What is important to note is that it is chiefly the individual's subjective perception of "risk" that plays a significant role in whether a situation is high risk or not. A high-risk situation poses a threat to one's perceived ability (what psychology calls "self-efficacy") to handle the challenging situation at hand (Greenfield et al., 2000). Therefore, by developing more effective coping skills, thereby increasing perceived self-efficacy, one can learn to manage a high-risk situation without defaulting to substance use (Earley, 1994).

Most relapse prevention guides provide various skills and tools for dealing with high-risk situations which are essential for sustained recovery. We assume that you already have these assets or are in the process of gaining them. Therefore, the focus of this workbook is not to provide an exhaustive set of relapse prevention skills and tools but to help you unlock your innate resilience so that you can effectively apply them. In this chapter and throughout the workbook, we focus on helping you to develop a **Recovery Resilience Practice**, which will enable you to use these assets to optimal effect. More specifically, you will learn about a mind-body system that, when overactive and not managed properly, hinders your capacity to effectively use your skills and tools to deal with high-risk situations or any troubling situation, thereby causing you to veer off your recovery pathway.

We begin with exercises that will help you to recognize when you are experiencing this mind-body system that acts as a hindrance, and to understand how it interferes with your ability to effectively navigate high-risk situations. Recognizing when this mind-body system is overactive is the first step in increasing your recovery resilience.

Experience the Hindrance

In Exercise 1.1 you will identify a situation that is currently causing you a great deal of trouble or distress (e.g., your current relationship or stress at work). You will use a template called a **Map** (see the example Map in Exercise 1.1). In this exercise you will perform **I-System Mapping**, or **Mapping** for short, a core Recovery Resilience Practice that helps you, through free association, recognize the mind-body system that acts as a hindrance to your innate resilience and interferes in your daily life.

Once you have identified a troubling situation, write it inside the oval on Map 1. Then take a couple of minutes to scatter your thoughts and feelings about that situation around the outside of the oval. Don't edit or second-guess; just write down whatever thoughts come to mind.

After a couple of minutes, stop writing, and at the bottom of the Map provide a description of your body tension. Where do you experience it in your body? How do you experience it?

Next, write the same troubling situation used in the Map 1 exercise you just completed in the oval of Map 2 in Exercise 1.2. Before you write anything else on the Map, take a few moments to tune into your senses.

Begin by getting comfortable in your chair and focusing on what you are currently doing. Next, just sit and listen to the background sounds. As you listen, feel your feet on the floor, the weight of your body on your seat. Feel the fabric of your clothing, or the tabletop, or just rub the tips of your fingers together while you continue to listen to the background sounds. If a thought distracts you, return to listening to the background sounds.

Once you begin to feel settled, write the thoughts and feelings that come to your mind now about the situation around the oval. As you write, feel the pen in your hand and watch the ink flow onto the paper while continually focusing on the background sounds. As with the previous Map, don't edit. There are no right or wrong thoughts. Just let your thoughts stream while you are tuned into your senses.

After a couple of minutes, stop writing and at the bottom of Map 2 provide a description of your body tension. Where do you experience it in your body? How do you experience it?

Now, compare Map 1 and Map 2. In the space in Exercise 1.3 write down a very brief description of your experience of doing Map 1, and then do the same for Map 2. The troubling situation in the oval is the same on both Maps, but what is different about your experience of the two Maps? What, if anything, has shifted for you? Write down your thoughts.

Example

Map 1

What if I cannot live
up to others'
expectations of me?

I have to give up
my life for this
job

I don't feel like going into
work today

Scared about
losing my job

Stress on the job

I will be never be
good enough

I don't know how to
manage my
supervisees at work

Anxious about
being so far
behind

What do I tell co-workers
when they disappoint or
frustrate me?

Description of body tension I feel so much tension in my neck & shoulders

Map 1

Description of body tension: _____

Map 2

Description of body tension: _____

Map 1	Map 2

Difference between Maps:

Did you experience more tension in Map 1 than in Map 2? Did you experience less stress and more lightness when completing Map 2? Was there more mental clutter in Map 1 than in Map 2? The answer to these questions is most likely "yes."

What caused the decrease in body tension and mental clutter? The reality of the situation did not change, but your orientation toward it did. When you did Map 1, you likely attributed all your distress to the troubling situation itself. But your body tension and mental clutter decreased when you did Map 2, even though the troubling situation is the same. So, if the troubling situation is not the sole cause of your distress, what is? This exercise demonstrates that there is something else besides the troubling situation that is causing your distress.

What you will discover as you complete this workbook is that excessive mental clutter (i.e., excessive worrying, rumination, obsessive thinking, and over-analyzing) and body tension are often signs that a certain mind-body state is prevailing and that this mind-body state is caused by a mind-body system. This mind-body system is operationalized as the **I-System** – a construct for a self-referential mind-body system that when overactive interferes with optimal functioning and innate resilience (Block et al., 2016). Your I-System was likely more active when you did Map 1 than it was when you did Map 2. Why? When you did Map 2, you literally "came to your senses" by focusing on the background sounds and your body sensations. Opening your awareness to what you are sensing quiets or "rests" your I-System.

When your I-System is overactive, it contracts your awareness and restricts your optimal functioning. These are the characteristics of the mind-body state called **I-System Functioning**. What does this have to do with your recovery? The I-System distorts how one perceives, thinks, feels, and acts. If not effectively managed, your I-System hinders your ability to draw on your recovery capital (skills and tools). What's more, it not only negatively affects your capacity to apply skills or tools, but it hinders all aspects of working a recovery program and living the good life.

As we outlined in the Introduction, the Recovery Resilience Program is based on the premise that we have an innate resilience toward growth and healing. You naturally experience and express this innate resilience when your I-System is rested and thus not hindering this access.

Excessive mental clutter and body tension are "red flags" that you are experiencing I-System Functioning. Learning to recognize when you are experiencing this mind-body state allows you to use the other Recovery Resilience Practices taught in this workbook to transform your I-System into a powerful ally.

Befriend Your I-System

In this section, you will learn how to transform your I-System from hindrance to helper and use it to help you stay on your recovery pathway instead of allowing it to make you veer off course. When you recognize that your I-System is active by noticing that you are experiencing mental clutter and body tension, you are using a Recovery Resilience Practice called **Recognize I-System Activity**. When you recognize that your I-System is overactive, it gives you an opportunity to befriend it.

You befriend your I-System when you recognize that its overactivity is causing you to go off course from living your best life and from tapping into your innate resources. The mental clutter and body tension you experience is a signal alerting you that your I-System is overactive. From now on, this signal can alert you that you are experiencing I-System Functioning and thus are not optimally prepared to deal with the situation at hand, so you can then act to correct course.

When you "came to your senses" while completing Map 2, you experienced this course correction – the shift in a mind-body state that occurred (i.e., from mental clutter and body tension to a lightness or calmness) when your I-System released its grip.

This shift is further illustrated through Exercise 1.4.

EXERCISE 1.4

As you sit in your chair, lean to the left or right for about 10 seconds, then bring yourself back to an upright centered position. When you leaned to the left or right, did you feel tension in your body? Did you feel a sense of imbalance? After you returned to an upright, centered position, did the body tension release? Did you feel more balanced?

Recognizing your I-System activity is like recognizing that you are tilting off-balance. The I-System alerts you to this imbalanced state. When you rest your I-System, you come back into balance. Simply put, the I-System creates this imbalanced state and sends signals alerting you that you are off course, and your Recovery Resilience Practice brings you back into balance. This shift, is referred to as the **Mind-Body Bridging Shift** (**the Shift** for short).

I-System Functioning inhibits optimal functioning by causing you to "get in your own way" as your thoughts turn inward and away from the task or moment at hand. When you are in this mind-body state, it distracts you from meeting the imperative of the moment and from drawing on your recovery capital and effectively applying your recovery skills. It is important to note that the I-System is not bad, as it plays an important function. Our aim is not to eliminate the I-System, which is not possible, but instead to make it an ally. Without awareness of its overactivity, it is counterproductive. With awareness, it acts as a compass that guides us in our activities of daily living.

Let's consider the example of a plane that has an automatic pilot system to illustrate how this works. As the plane flies toward its destination, the automatic pilot self-corrects, moment to moment, to keep the plane on course regardless of the conditions. In the same way, each time you befriend your I-System and experience the Shift, you correct course and stay true to your recovery pathway and life goals.

Your Optimal State

Look at Map 2 (Exercise 1.2) again. Even though the situation was the same, you likely had a different experience while doing this Map. When focused on the background sounds and your body sensations, your I-System quietened or was rested, your mental clutter and body tension reduced, and you most likely had a different perspective of the situation. The reality of the troubling situation did not change, but your orientation toward it did because you shifted toward a more expansive mind-body state.

In doing Map 2, you likely shifted to a mind-body state termed **Natural Functioning**. Natural Functioning refers to our state or mode of being when focused on the present moment or activity *without the hindrance* of the I-System. Because it is your natural mind-body state, Natural Functioning spontaneously arises when you rest your I-System. When you shifted to Natural Functioning, you were brought back into balance. Although there is often little we can do about external events, there is often a great deal we can do about our internal orientation to the event or situation. When you recognize that your I-System is overactive when dealing with any situation and you take action to rest it, you are less at the mercy of the external event or situation and naturally more confident in your ability to cope with it.

One of the central premises of the Recovery Resilience Program is that in a Natural Functioning state we are more resourceful and resilient, and we can tap into our innate capacity for flourishing. This point of view is shared by several scholars who assert that we have an innate resilience and drive toward self-actualization (sometimes referred to as the "true" or "real" self). The psychoanalyst Karen Horney (1950) proposed that the "real" self contains potential for growth, happiness, and willpower, and for achieving self-actualization. These scholars postulate that growth and flourishing spontaneously occur if one removes what hinders it from manifesting (Danielian & Gianotti, 2012, 2017; Horney, 1950). For example, plants have an innate capacity to grow when one places them in the right environment. They cannot be forced to grow. One can only create the right conditions for growth to occur. In this regard humans are not that dissimilar – when we access our natural resourcefulness we flourish.

The aim of developing a Recovery Resilience Practice is to simply remove the I-System's interference from our innate resourcefulness, resilience, and capacity for flourishing. We can therefore see that it is not just the **"what"** and **"how"** that comprise an effective and sustainable recovery lifestyle but also the **"who"** that is doing it. The "who" that is engaged in your recovery is the essence of building recovery resilience. The "who" is as equally important as the "what." There are many books and programs on "what" to do for a sustainable recovery, but the Recovery Resilience Program and this workbook focus primarily on "who" is doing it – your Natural Functioning self or your I-System Functioning self.

Our approach is based on the premise that your Natural Functioning mind-body state is central to achieving what the Greek philosopher Aristotle called *eudaimonia*, often translated as *flourishing*.[2] In a Natural Functioning mind-body state, we meet the imperative of each moment without the hindrance of an overactive I-System. We automatically tap into our innate resources. This does not mean we act or behave perfectly, but we do our best, at that moment, unfettered by the I-System's interference. In Natural Functioning we are capable of *phronesis*, an ancient Greek word for a type of wisdom or intelligence relevant to practical action. In our Natural Functioning mind-body state, we have access to our innate resilience, our various recovery skills and tools (recovery capital), and the practical wisdom (*phronesis*) to meet the demands of the moment.

I-System Requirements

Now you may ask, what triggers the I-System to become overactive and create this imbalanced state that causes you to get in your own way, impedes your capacity to work a recovery program, and makes you veer off your recovery pathway? This is an important question, and we are going to explore it by doing two Mapping exercises. First, you will complete a *How I Would Like Certain People to Act* Map followed by a *How I Would Like to Be* Map.

For the *How I Would Like Certain People to Act* Map, write down inside the circle in Exercise 1.5 how you would like certain important people in your life to act or behave. Then draw a line to the outside of the circle and write down each person's behavior when they contradict how you would like them to act. Then, for each of the items outside the circle, write down the degree of your body tension and the degree of negative emotional response. Note it on a scale from 1 (low) to 3 (high). Refer to the example Map provided in Exercise 1.5.

Example

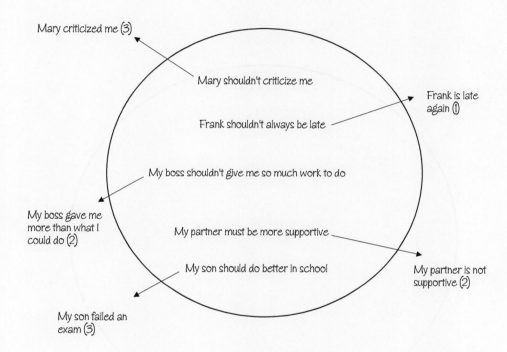

How I Would Like Certain People to Act Map

Mary criticized me (3)

Mary shouldn't criticize me

Frank is late again (1)

Frank shouldn't always be late

My boss shouldn't give me so much work to do

My boss gave me more than what I could do (2)

My partner must be more supportive

My son should do better in school

My partner is not supportive (2)

My son failed an exam (3)

How I Would Like Certain People to Act Map

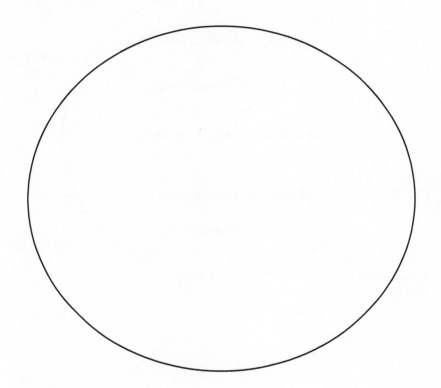

Note that on this *How I Would Like Certain People to Act* Map the items inside the circle may be natural expectations you have for that person. However, if you normally have a lot of mental clutter and body tension in response to that person's behavior outside the circle, it is your sign that your I-System becomes overactive when they behave like that.

We all have expectations. When some of these are violated, it does not bother us much, if at all. But when some expectations are not met, we experience significant mental clutter and body tension, as you may have noticed when completing the exercise. When you experience significant mental clutter and body tension when an expectation is not met, it is a sign that the unmet expectation has triggered your I-System. We refer to these type of expectations as **I-System Requirements** or **Requirements** for short. They are what cause your I-System to become overactive and interfere with your Natural Functioning.

Requirements are simply the "shoulds" or "musts" we have about a particular situation. The I-System generates Requirements each moment of how you, others, or the world absolutely should or must be. When you have a violated Requirement (i.e., reality does not conform to your Requirement), your I-System becomes overactive.

Why do Requirements over-activate the I-System? We will use an analogy to explain. All living systems strive to maintain homeostasis. When your body does not feel right, it instinctively self-regulates to restore its optimal functioning. For example, when your body temperature is too high, you sweat, and if it goes too low, you shiver. Your temperature-regulating system automatically tries to stabalize your body's optimal temperature. Analogously, your I-System, instead of working to maintain an ideal and stable temperature, works to maintain an ideal and stable view of yourself, others and the world. The reason that these "ideal pictures" or "mental rules" (I-System Requirements) of how you, others, and the world should or absolutely must be cause you distress when they are not realized is simply because they relate to your identity or self-concept. Hence the name I-System. So, when a Requirement is violated, it is not merely experienced as a minor disappointment, but rather as a direct threat to "who you think you are." Karen Horney (1950) referred to these type of demands as a "tyranny of shoulds."

There are many factors that influence our self-concept or "who we think we are," including certain beliefs about others and the world. When you experience excessive body tension and mental clutter (signs of I-System Functioning), you can bet that something is not conforming to the Requirements you have for yourself, others, or the world. When you recognize that a Requirement has triggered your I-System, you are practicing a Recovery Resilience Practice called **Recognize Requirements**.

Now let's do another exercise to further illustrate the concept of Requirements. For the next exercise, you will do a *How I Would Like to Be* Map. For this Map in Exercise 1.6 write down the qualities you wish to have. Write five of these qualities inside the circle. Then draw a line to the outside of the circle and write down the opposite of that quality. Now for each of the qualities outside the circle, consider the degree of body tension and negative emotional response you experience when you display these qualities. Refer to the example Map in Exercise 1.6.

Like the previous Map, all the qualities inside the circle may be natural expectations you have for yourself. But, if you have excessive mental clutter and body tension associated with the qualities outside the circle, it is a sign that they trigger your I-System. As mentioned, what activates your I-System are the Requirements inside the circle. For example, wanting to be successful is a natural expectation. However, when you fail (or feel as if you're failing) and you have mental clutter and body tension, it signifies that it is a Requirement, "I should be successful." That means that your ability to deal with the present moment is impaired because your I-System is overactive and interfering with your Natural Functioning. Simply recognizing that a Requirement has activated your I-System helps you experience the shift to Natural Functioning.

As was previously mentioned, Recovery Resilience Practice does not focus on changing any given situation (the "what") (crucial insofar as many distressful situations or triggers may be unavoidable) but instead focuses on changing the "who" that is dealing with the situation. In *It Works How and Why: The Twelve Steps and Twelve Traditions of Narcotics Anonymous* it states: "It is a spiritual axiom that whenever we are disturbed, no matter the cause, there is something wrong with us" (Narcotics Anonymous World Services, 1983, p. 92). This is exactly what the I-System leads us to believe, that it is the "what" that's the problem. What we are attempting to point

Example

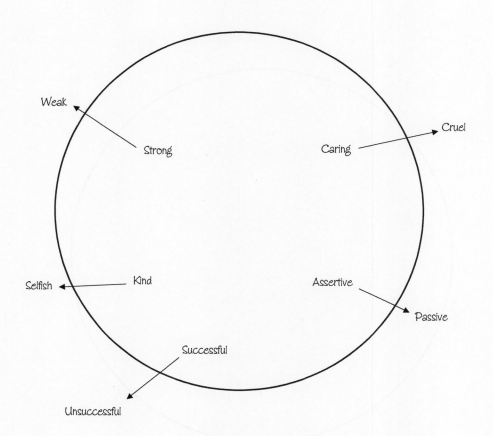

How I Would Like to Be Map

Weak ← Strong

Cruel ← Caring

Selfish ← Kind

Assertive → Passive

Successful → Unsuccessful

How I Would Like to Be Map

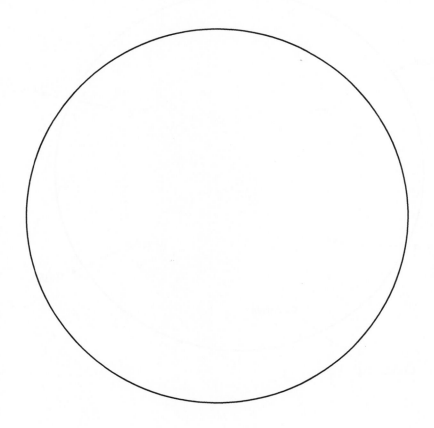

out is that it is not the "what" (situation) that distresses us – which, by the way, may not be amenable to change – but rather the "who" that is dealing with the "what." That is, when we deal with any situation or moment in I-System Functioning, we will experience body tension and mental clutter and have limited access to our recovery capital. When we deal with these "whats" in Natural Functioning, we have more access to our recovery capital and skills. Recognizing when a Requirement has activated your I-System is critical to making sure the right "who" that is best equipped to stay on the recovery path is in charge. The Stoic philosopher Epictetus highlights this point of view by stating, "It's not what happens to you, but how you react to it that matters" (Taylor, 2021, p. 220). We would modify the second part of this statement slightly to "... but the 'who' that reacts to it that matters."

Choosing to use Recognize Requirements and other Recovery Resilience Practices to rest your I-System allows you to experience your innate resilience moment by moment and to live your best life. Making the same, basic point, this time from an existential perspective, psychiatrist and Holocaust survivor Dr. Viktor Frankl asserted: "Everything can be taken from a man but one thing: the last of the human freedoms – to choose one's attitude in any given set of circumstances, to choose one's own way" (Frankl, 1969, p. 86). You can simply choose to befriend your I-System and use it as a guide as you travel on your recovery pathway, or you can choose to let it veer you off course – it is up to you.

Now let's see how what you've learned and experienced so far relates to high-risk situations.

High-Risk Situations

Each person has a unique set of high-risk situations related to his or her life and experience of addiction. Even so, there are nevertheless three generally agreed upon categories that most high-risk situations fit within: (1) negative or challenging internal, emotional states; (2) external social pressure; and (3) interpersonal conflict.[3] As an individual in recovery, it is impossible to avoid all high-risk situations and their associated internal or external triggers. It is imperative, however, for the sake of ongoing sobriety, to learn to effectively manage these situations by managing the "who" that is dealing with them.

In the following exercise you will make a list of potential high-risk situations using the three categories:

- intrapersonal (which take place internally, within yourself, for example, your attitudes, thinking, and emotional states);
- interpersonal (refers to things taking place between people, for example, your relationship with your partner); and
- environmental (e.g., external stressors such as finances, work, and social events).

It is not important at this stage to be comprehensive in your list; rather, it's important that you start with those items which are "on the front burner" or uppermost in your mind. As with most of the exercises in this workbook, we provide some examples.

High-risk situations		
Intrapersonal (self)	**Interpersonal (others)**	**Environmental (the world)**
Self-pity	Arguing with partner	Social event

For this next exercise, you will once again use a Map template. As previously introduced, Mapping is a core Recovery Resilience Practice that helps you, through free association, recognize your I-System activity. The central aim of Mapping is to help you "see" how your I-System works and interferes in your daily life including your ability to handle high-risk situations when you encounter them.

For this exercise, you will choose one of the high-risk situations from the list you created in the previous exercise and write it inside the oval of Map 1 in Exercise 1.8. Then take a couple of minutes to scatter your thoughts and feelings about that situation around the outside of the oval. Don't edit or second-guess; just write down whatever thoughts come to mind. An example of how to do this is provided on the next page.

After a couple of minutes, stop writing and at the bottom of Map 1 provide a description of your body tension. Where do you experience it in your body? How do you experience it?

On the next Map in Exercise 1.9, write the same high-risk situation used in Map 1 of Exercise 1.8 in the oval.

Begin by first getting comfortable in your chair and focusing on what you are currently doing. Next, just sit and listen to the background sounds. As you listen, feel your feet on the floor, the weight of your body on your seat. Feel the fabric of your clothing, or the tabletop, or just rub the tips of your fingers together while you continue to listen to the background sounds. If a thought distracts you, return to listening to the background sounds.

Once you begin to feel settled, write the thoughts and feelings that come to your mind now about the situation around the oval. As you write, feel the pen in your hand and watch the ink flow onto the paper while continually focusing on the background sounds. As with the previous Map, don't edit. There are no right or wrong thoughts. Just let your thoughts stream while you are tuned into your senses.

After a couple of minutes, stop writing and at the bottom of Map 2 provide a description of your body tension. Where do you experience it in your body? How do you experience it?

Now, compare Map 1 and Map 2. In the space below in Exercise 1.9, write down a very brief description of your experience of doing Map 1, and then do the same for Map 2. The situation in the oval is the same on both Maps, but what is different about your experience of the two Maps? What, if anything, has shifted for you? Write down your thoughts.

Example

High-Risk Situation Map 1

What if somebody
offers me alcohol?

It will be boring
sober

I don't feel like going.

Scared

Holiday Party at Work

I will be socially awkward

I don't know how to socialize sober

Anxious

What do I tell people when
they offer me a drink?

Description of body tension? <u>Butterflies in stomach</u>

High-Risk Situation Map 1

Description of body tension: _____

High-Risk Situation Map 2

Description of body tension: _____

Map 1	Map 2

Difference between Maps:

As with the previous troubling situation Map exercise (Exercise 1.1), did you experience more tension in Map 1 than in Map 2? Did you experience less stress and more lightness when completing Map 2? Was there more mental clutter in Map 1 than in Map 2?

The high-risk situation did not change, but your orientation toward it probably did. When you did Map 1, you likely attributed all your distress to the high-risk situation itself. But your body tension and mental clutter decreased when you did Map 2, even though the troubling situation is the same. This exercise again demonstrates that there is something else (your I-System) besides the high-risk situation that is causing your distress.

Map 1 helps you see that when there is I-System activity it makes it even more difficult to manage a high-risk situation. This is because when you attempt to deal with a high-risk situation or any troubling, stressful, or painful situation in I-System Functioning it limits your awareness and ability to act optimally. When your I-System is active, it hinders your ability to draw on your recovery capital and skills and thereby limits your choices to a few habitual behaviors.

And for those struggling with addiction, relapse is often the default response when confronted with stressful, painful, high-risk, and troubling situations.

In Map 2 you likely experienced some release from I-System Functioning (i.e., the Shift). When you remove this hindrance, your capacity to effectively deal with high-risk situations dramatically increases because you have more capacity to access your recovery capital and skills.

Earlier in this chapter, you learned that I-System Functioning inhibits optimal functioning by causing you to "get in your own way" as your thoughts turn inward and away from the task or moment at hand and that when you are in this mind-body state it keeps you from meeting the imperative of the moment optimally. Remember that the I-System is not bad, as it plays an important function. You only need to learn to befriend it, which requires that you are aware of when it is active. Doing this transforms the I-System from a hindrance to a compass that tells you when you are getting off track and guides you back to Natural Functioning.

In Exercise 1.11, we are going to look for the Requirements associated with a high-risk situation that overactivate your I-System when they are violated.

Go back to Map 1 (Exercise 1.8) and circle the thoughts on the Map that cause a great deal of mental clutter and body tension. Then ask yourself how you would like these items to be. Sometimes the Requirement is as simple as being the opposite of the thought on the Map (see the Example 1.10 on the next page: *I don't know how to socialize sober -> I should know how to socialize sober*); other times you can identify a Requirement by asking the question "What is my Requirement for this situation?"

Write the thoughts you circled as "should" or "must" statements. Connect each circled thought to its "should" or "must" statement with a line (see example Map of Exercise 1.10: Thought: *What if somebody offers me alcohol? ->* Requirement: *Someone should not offer me alcohol*). You may have written some of the thoughts on your Map as "should" or "must" statements. If you did, just circle them (see example Map of Exercise 1.10: Thought: *I shouldn't be anxious*).

As previously mentioned, when you realize that a Requirement has been violated and has triggered your I-System, you are using a Recovery Resilience Practice called **Recognize Requirements**. The aim of this practice is to become aware when a Requirement has been violated as you go through your daily activities. When you become aware of a Requirement, it causes it to lose power to keep your I-System overactive. For example, let's say you have a Requirement

Example

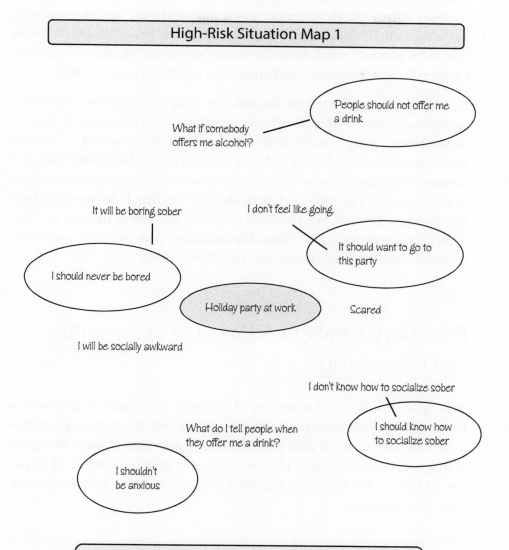

High-Risk Situation Map 1

People should not offer me a drink

What if somebody offers me alcohol?

It will be boring sober

I don't feel like going.

I should never be bored

It should want to go to this party

Holiday party at work

Scared

I will be socially awkward

I don't know how to socialize sober

What do I tell people when they offer me a drink?

I should know how to socialize sober

I shouldn't be anxious

Description of body tension? <u>Butterflies in stomach</u>

that *"Life should be fair."* When you experience unfairness in some way or another, you will notice body tension and mental clutter, which are signs of I-System activity. When you notice these mind and body signals, you simply say to yourself, *"I have a Requirement that life should be fair."* Doing this in the heat of the moment, when the Requirement is violated, initiates the shift from I-System Functioning to Natural Functioning and quiets your I-System.

As you have learned, it is not the situation (the "what") that causes your I-System to become active, but rather the Requirements we (often automatically and out of awareness) have regarding that situation. It is frequently a violated Requirement associated with a high-risk situation that makes it more difficult to manage. Why? Because when the violated Requirement triggers your I-System, your awareness and optimal functioning are restricted. Recognizing your Requirements for high-risk situations will make it easier to manage the situation because you will do it in Natural Functioning where you can draw on your recovery capital and skills to deal with the situation more effectively.

Recovery Resilience Practice in Activities of Daily Living

Now let's look at some examples of how you can apply your Recovery Resilience Practice throughout the day. As we will stress throughout this workbook, the arena of your practice is your **activities of daily living**. As highlighted, your I-System is like a compass that provides a signal when you are off course. The following examples illustrate how this moment by moment practice works.

Example

Situation: Taking a shower in the morning while clenching your jaws and having thoughts on how hard the day is going to be.

Signal: Clenched jaws and negative thoughts on how hard the day is going to be.

My Requirement(s): "The day should be easy." "I should have more time for myself." "I shouldn't have to deal with hard days."

Example

Situation: Getting dressed and experiencing a racing heart rate with thoughts of you not looking good enough in your clothes.

Signal: Racing heart and negative thoughts of how you don't look good enough and also experiencing cravings.

My Requirement(s): "The outfit should be perfect." "I should look good in my outfits." "I should always look my best." "People should accept me and my outfit choices."

Example

Situation: Getting an unexpected email at work about how you made a mistake and experiencing a tight chest while having thoughts of how you're failing.

Signal: Tight chest and thoughts of being a failure. Thoughts of wanting to drink.

My Requirement(s): "I should never make mistakes." "I shouldn't fail." "People should understand me." "People should be respectful."

Recognizing your Requirements doesn't make the situation better or erase mistakes of the past. However, it allows you to break free from the box the I-System puts you in and leads to the benefits of Natural Functioning, which permits you to optimally handle the situation at hand and move forward with your day.

Sensory Awareness

When you completed Map 2 in the previous exercises (Exercises 1.2, 1.9), you likely experienced a shift from I-System Functioning to Natural Functioning, even though the troubling situation or high-risk situation was the same as the one on Map 1 (Exercises 1.1, 1.8). What caused this shift? Simply put, when you

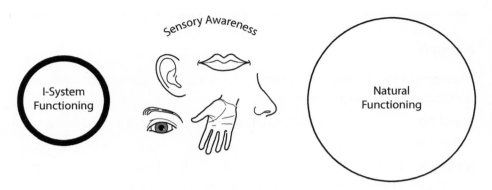

Figure 1 Sensory awareness skills.

completed Map 2 you literally "came to your senses" by focusing on the background sounds and your body sensations. When tuned into your senses the I-System automatically quiets and your mental clutter and body tension decrease. You shift from a limited and contracted state of being to a more expanded, flexible, and resilient state of being. You don't have to stretch to move into Natural Functioning because it happens automatically when you rest your I-System.

When you did Map 2 in Exercises 1.2 and 1.9 you were performing a Recovery Resilience Practice called **Sensory Awareness**. It is as easy as listening attentively to the sound of an air conditioner, traffic outside, water going down the drain when you wash your hands, or the sound of a clock ticking. Anytime in the day when you recognize that your I-System has become overactive, practice Sensory Awareness to initiate the Shift. This is particularly useful in high-risk situations, as it will help you deal with the situation in Natural Functioning.

It is important to note that sometimes when you experience excessive or overwhelming I-System activity (this happens to all of us), applying Sensory Awareness will not necessarily completely quiet I-System activity. But with consistent practice, in the long run, you will find it to be a helpful component of your Recovery Resilience Practice.

Below is a list of various types of Sensory Awareness which you can practice throughout the day to quiet your I-System:

Awareness of Background Sounds
Your environment is full of sounds. During the day, pause and listen to background sounds, like the white noise of the heating or air-conditioning system, the wind blowing, traffic sounds, or the hum of the refrigerator.

Awareness of What You Are Touching

Be aware of what your fingers sense as you touch things like glasses, phones, pens, keys, computers, and other objects. Are these surfaces smooth or rough, cold or warm, pleasant or unpleasant? Sense what it's like to feel the sun's warmth on your face or the breeze on your skin.

Awareness of Colors and Shapes

Pay attention today to what you see when you look at scenery and objects. Notice their colors, shapes, and forms.

Awareness of Your Body

Because of the unpleasant body sensations often associated with your overactive I-System, you may have developed a habit of trying to block out or get away from the feelings in your body. Pay attention to various bodily sensations or any tension or emotions experienced in the body. When you walk, feel the sensation of your feet touching the ground. When you sit, feel the pressure of the chair against your body.

Just for Today

In Twelve-Step fellowships, members are advised to live "Just for Today." The practice of Sensory Awareness increases our capacity to live "Just for Today." Contrarily, active addiction brings with it a kind of "mindlessness," in which attention is distractible, a sense of purpose inaccessible, where being in the present moment is encumbered by cravings and/or withdrawal – and shame and self-judgment are the order of the day (Creswell et al., 2007; Teyber et al., 2011). On top of this, active addicts often apply ineffective and maladaptive coping strategies in stressful and troubling life situations. Sensory Awareness and being present in the moment provide an alternative (Natural Functioning) for coping with stress, negative affect, and anxiety.[4] In the context of addiction, Sensory Awareness means "becoming aware of triggers for craving ... and choosing to do something else which might ameliorate or prevent craving, so weakening this habitual response" (Groves & Farmer, 1994, p. 189).

The practice of Sensory Awareness temporarily rests the I-System, thereby facilitating recovery resilience. It increases and expands our awareness, a necessary aptitude in recovery because activity without awareness is a feature of impulsive, mood-dependent, and addictive behavior (Lazarus & Folkman, 1984). Sensory Awareness is a way of cultivating and strengthening this awareness (Nakamura et al., 2015). Addiction over a period of time distorts our view of reality. More specifically, the defense mechanism of denial, which is one of the primary obstacles to initiating and sustaining successful recovery, is itself a profound narrowing of awareness. This in turn leads to a fragmented understanding of the widespread damage that goes hand in hand with addiction, which then only perpetuates the negative, addictive cycle. As Gestalt psychology pioneer Fritz Perls (1969, p. 66) put it: "Without awareness there is no cognition of choice." Conversely, with increased awareness there is increased choice, and consequently increased ability to break the cycle of addiction. When your I-System is overactive, your awareness contracts, leading to a more distorted and limited view of reality. When we practice Sensory Awareness and experience the Shift a more balanced awareness expands spontaneously, which leads to a more comprehensive point of view that allows us to see things as they really are, and thus to a better insight into the true nature of our addiction and the consequences of using substances.

The practice of Sensory Awareness can also lead to greater acceptance of one's internal experiences. In the context of the above discussion, it leads to greater acceptance of cravings or other painful feeling states rather than counterproductive shaming and self-judgment. Enhanced coping may also be experienced as the capacity for intentional inaction, which can be described as a "letting go" and not acting on a craving or impulse to try to "fix" the negative feeling (The Asian wisdom traditions speak similarly of "actionless action," or *wu wei*.). From this perspective, the focus is on identifying and accepting the craving, thought, or feeling, not acting on it or attempting to fight it or *fix* it. This is sometimes referred to as "urge surfing" in relapse prevention programs. Instead of trying to eliminate the urge, one surfs it as one would surf a wave, until it naturally fades away. Cravings only last for a certain period of time and will eventually run out of steam if they are not attended to.

It must be noted that Sensory Awareness skills differ from other mindfulness-based interventions (Bowen et al., 2011) that also practice tuning into the senses, in that the aim is not to merely have a detached awareness of our thoughts but to understand the workings of our mind (in psychology this is called metacognition – simply meaning, thinking about thinking).[5] We want to also label specific I-System thoughts and the various I-System narratives or stories. So instead of merely observing thoughts with detached awareness, we also want to be thinking about our thinking, and therefore "befriend" the various components of our I-Systems. Sensory Awareness is an important practice as it initiates a shift from I-System Functioning to Natural Functioning; however, on its own it is not sufficient. What is additionally required is an awareness of the components of your I-System which is the focus of the other Recovery Resilience Practices introduced later in the workbook.

Something we will stress throughout this workbook is that it is not the exercises herein that are your Recovery Resilience Practice but how you apply the practices in each moment of daily living – just for today. At the beginning of your practice, it may feel awkward and mechanical, but with more practice, it will become second nature. Like in Twelve-Step programs where participants are urged to apply the spiritual principles of the program in all their affairs, we suggest that a Recovery Resilience Practice is aimed at relating to all your activities in a state of Natural Functioning. When befriending the I-System, it will act as a guide and compass alerting you when any of its Requirements have been violated, thus giving you an opportunity to shift to relating to the situation in Natural Functioning, with expanded awareness and more practical wisdom and practical reasoning. Your practice hall or dojo is each moment.

I-System Functioning results in limited options for dealing with life because it restricts our capacity to use our recovery capital. It fundamentally results in a lack of creativity. The famous psychoanalytic thinker Otto Rank argued that most of life's problems are due to a lack of creativity.[6] From the I-System Model perspective we can see that Requirements limit our choices to those that are only congruent with our Requirements. When encumbered by Requirements we have limited creativity to deal optimally with each moment in daily living and remain weighted down and boxed in them. In Natural Functioning, we do not have to force ourselves to be creative because in this state we are automatically creative and resourceful in the sense that the options we now have are expanded beyond those imposed on us by our I-System's "tyranny of shoulds."

Well done for completing Chapter 1 of the workbook! On the next page we provide an overview of the practices introduced in Chapter 1.

OVERVIEW OF CHAPTER 1

Recovery Resilience Practice

- Do **Mapping** related to any high-risk situation or troubling experience.
- **Recognize I-System Activity** by being aware of body tension and mental clutter.
- Practice **Sensory Awareness**.
- **Recognize Requirements** when performing daily activities.
- **Experience the Shift** as you move from I-System Functioning to Natural Functioning.

At the end of each chapter, we include certain scales and templates which will assist you in developing a Recovery Resilience practice.

On the next few pages please fill out the following:

Flourishing Scale: Complete the scale and calculate your score, from 1 to 7, for each question over the past week or two. The Flourishing Scale will provide a measure to help you track your progress as you work through this workbook and develop a Recovery Resilience Practice. The Flourishing Scale is designed to measure your subjective happiness, well-being, and quality of life. The same scale is included at the end of each chapter of the workbook.

Recovery Resilience Practice Scale: Complete the scale and calculate and write down the frequency of your Recovery Resilience Practice. Indicate whether it was never, hardly ever, occasionally, or regularly. The same scale is included at the end of each chapter of the workbook.

We recommend practicing what was outlined in this chapter for 1–2 weeks before moving on to the next chapter. As you incorporate your Recovery Resilience Practice into your life, it will feel more natural and instinctive. And remember "progress not perfection."

Flourishing Scale

Date: _____

Below are eight statements with which you may agree or disagree. Using the 1–7 scale below, indicate your agreement with each item by indicating that response for each statement.

- 7 – Strongly agree
- 6 – Agree
- 5 – Slightly agree
- 4 – Neither agree nor disagree
- 3 – Slightly disagree
- 2 – Disagree
- 1 – Strongly disagree

Indicate your agreement with each item	(1–7)
I lead a purposeful and meaningful life	
My social relationships are supportive and rewarding	
I am engaged and interested in my daily activities	
I actively contribute to the happiness and well-being of others	
I am competent and capable in the activities that are important to me	
I am a good person and live a good life	
I am optimistic about my future	
People respect me	
Total score:	_____

The *Flourishing Scale* was developed by Diener, E., Wirtz, D., Tov, W., et al. (2010). New measures of well-being: Flourishing and positive and negative feelings. *Social Indicators Research, 39,* 247–266.

Recovery Resilience Practice Scale

Date: _____

Over the past week indicate the frequency of your Recovery Resilience Practice. Check the description that most closely reflects your practice: never, hardly ever, or occasionally.

Frequency of Resilient Resilience Practice	Never	Hardly Ever	Occasionally	Regularly
Recognize I-System Activity				
Mapping				
Recognize Requirements				
Sensory Awareness				
Experience the Shift				

2
• • • • • • • • • •

Coping with Cravings
and Triggers

*I want to learn more and more to see as beautiful what is necessary in
things; then I shall be one of those who make things beautiful.*
Friedrich Nietzsche, *The Joyful Science*

Addictive behavior can be understood as being part of a mode of being,
meaning that it is a particular and habitual way of existing, relating, and living. Your **addicted mode of being** (or **addicted mode** for short) refers to all
your beliefs, thoughts, attitudes, and fantasies that support your addictive
behavior over time. An addicted mode can also be understood as a particular
mind-body state that accompanies all addictive behavior. Once you enter an
addicted mode, your awareness, attitudes, and behavior contract to the habitual patterns of your addicted lifestyle. Anyone who has experienced addiction to substances will relate to the notion that the act of using is merely
one aspect of their addictive lifestyle. The premise of this workbook is that
your addicted mode is one of many possible dysfunctional mind-body states
or modes of being you can experience when your I-System is overactive
(Block et al., 2016).

Your addicted mode is not a permanent or chronic condition, but rather a tran-
sitory mode that is one of many possible modes of being (healthy or dysfunctional). Your addicted mode can be understood as a **disposition**, in the sense

that it is not always active or present, but rather a state you enter under certain conditions (it is context-dependent) – that is, when your I-System is overactive. Natural Functioning can also be viewed from this perspective. It is a state you automatically experience when your I-System is resting. Addiction can be seen as a way of life that has been taken hostage by a particular mode of being.

An example of a disposition is a vase standing on a table. It has a disposition to break under certain conditions, such as if it gets bumped off the table and lands on a hard floor. Therefore, it has a disposition for two possible states, that is, being whole or being broken (under certain conditions). In the same way, one can have a disposition for inhabiting an addicted mode and addictive behavior, and as we will highlight in the workbook, there are some conditions or contexts that can activate this disposition. By learning how to rest your I-System, you can influence this disposition.

Your addicted mode and Natural Functioning mode are two distinct modes of being, each with its unique characteristics. You can only inhabit one of these modes at a time. When you rest your overactive I-System and consequently move into a Natural Functioning mode, it lessens the power of the beliefs, expectations, thoughts, fantasies, and attitudes that comprise your addicted mode. In your Natural Functioning mode, the possibility of relapse decreases significantly.

Cravings

It is often stated that cravings are a formidable adversary to those on a recovery pathway and that cravings are one of the major factors related to relapse (Brewer, 2017; Marlatt, 1985). From an addiction treatment perspective, the management of cravings is a primary goal both in psychotherapy and pharmacotherapy. Individuals who lack effective coping responses and/or the confidence (self-efficacy) to deal with cravings and the situations that trigger them are at high risk for relapse (Miller et al., 1996). Consequently, your ability to manage cravings is a pivotal coping skill needed for your sustained recovery from addiction (Ahmed & Pickards, 2019).

Craving is often part of the habitual thoughts, emotions, attitudes, beliefs, and fantasies of an addicted mode. But cravings are also something we naturally experience. Some cravings are imperative for our survival. For example, if you did not crave water when your body needs water you could die. Cravings can also be a sign that our needs are not being met. Hence the acronym, inspired by a shorter version often used in Twelve-Step communities, of *HAALT-BB* (hungry, angry, anxious, lonely, tired, bored, and blue), which signifies certain emotional states and needs that when not met can lead to cravings. In any case, they are a natural and unavoidable aspect of any recovery process.

Cravings are best understood as existing on a continuum. On the one side are cravings that naturally arise and fade. On the other side are cravings that are amplified in various degrees of intensity when they are experienced in the addicted mode due to an overactive I-System. When one experiences cravings in an addicted mode, which limits access to one's recovery capital, the cravings can seem overwhelming.

This workbook is based on the idea that in a Natural Functioning mind-body state or mode, you will better handle your cravings than you will in an addicted mode (overactive I-System mind-body state). To explain this metaphorically we will use two vessels – a one-ounce vessel and a twenty-ounce vessel (see Figure 1) to represent your internal experience of cravings and your mode of being. Imagine the one-ounce vessel is filled to the top with cravings – this represents being in an addicted mode with an overactive I-System. This vessel is so full that there is no room for your recovery capital. Your existence is limited to relating to yourself, others, and the world only

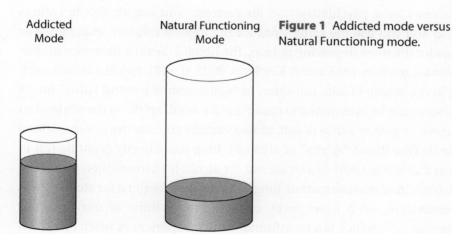

Addicted
Mode

Natural Functioning
Mode

Figure 1 Addicted mode versus Natural Functioning mode.

through the perspective of this addicted mode. In this overactive I-System mind-body state, overwhelmed by your cravings, you experience yourself as limited, and trapped within this addicted mode. You are cut off from your recovery capital and, consequently, your ability to handle cravings (the empty space in Figure 1) is greatly limited.

When you rest your overactive I-System, you expand your internal capacity and mode of being. Metaphorically speaking, it's like pouring your "one ounce of cravings" into a twenty-ounce vessel. Even though the same "amount" of cravings are present, they don't seem overwhelming. This is because in this Natural Functioning mind-body state – who you are without I-System interference – your innate resilience spontaneously emerges; you have full access to your recovery capital. The situation and cravings haven't changed, but your capacity to deal with them has increased. There is more space in the container, which represents a greater capacity to deal with the situation.

In Natural Functioning, the state of being which is symbolized in Figure 1 by the bigger vessel, you have expanded your sense of self and mode of being beyond your self-centered addicted mode. In the "Big Book" of Alcoholics Anonymous, it is stated that at the root of alcoholism is self-centered fear (Wilson, 1976). This contracted and limited addicted mode of self-centered fear (you in the small vessel) is caused by your overactive I-System. In this self-centered state, you come to falsely believe that your addicted mode and its cravings and habitual behavior are who you are.

In a letter addressed to Bill Wilson, the cofounder of Alcoholics Anonymous, the famous Swiss psychiatrist Carl Jung wrote: "You see, alcohol in Latin is *spiritus* and you use the same word for the highest religious experience as well as for the most depraving poison. The helpful formula therefore is: *spiritus contra spiritum* (in Kurtz & Ketcham, 2002, p. 118). *Spiritus contra spiritum*, in the original Latin, translates as "spirit against [*contra*] spirit." Jung's suggestion can be interpreted to mean that we need "spirit" in the sense of an enlarged, or greater sense of self, to successfully counter the lesser spiritual facsimile (the literal "spirits" of alcohol). Jung was directly pointing out to Wilson that at the heart of a treatment for alcoholism there often is an existential/spiritual transformation. Jung believed that the thirst for alcohol "was the equivalent, on a lower level, of the spiritual thirst of our being for wholeness ... " – which is a transformation one experiences when one shifts from the limited, isolated, and self-centered "I" of the addicted mode (overactive I-System mind-body state) to the wholeness and interconnectedness found in one's Natural Functioning mind-body state or mode. This shift is illustrated in the epigraph of this chapter: "I want to learn more and more to see as beautiful what is necessary in things; then I shall be one of those who make things beautiful" (Nietzsche, 2003, p. 157).

Triggers

We will now explore triggers, which are social, environmental, or emotional cues that remind people in recovery of their past drug or alcohol use. These cues bring about cravings that may lead to a relapse. One can often choose to avoid certain high-risk situations, but it is impossible to avoid all triggers.

Triggers can be external or internal. External triggers are people, places, activities, and objects that elicit thoughts or cravings associated with substance use. Internal triggers involve feelings, thoughts, or emotions formerly associated with substance use. Both external and internal triggers are related to past experiences of substance use that can lead to cravings. For example, when an alcoholic drives past a bar, the experience of seeing the bar is an external trigger that leads to a craving for alcohol. Similarly, when a cocaine addict feels lonely and bored, these emotions associated with past cocaine use are an internal trigger that leads to a craving for cocaine. In both examples, the use of substances is governed by reinforcement principles and has a direct effect on the pleasure centers of the brain (Bell et al., 2014; Polk, 2015).[1] The euphoria produced by the stimulation of the pleasure center by drug use tends to positively reinforce addictive behavior and its associated triggers. Therefore, any trigger related to past positive experiences of using substances and/or an internal state of mind or emotion can lead to intense cravings and memories of positive substance use experiences. As a result, the resumption of addictive behavior or substance use may be prompted by situational cues and/or internal, emotional triggers. Therefore, acquiring and using coping skills for dealing with cravings that result from triggers is central to a sustained recovery.

Like the exercise of identifying high-risk situations in Chapter 1, you will now make a list of potential triggers. Make a list of intrapersonal (e.g., your thoughts, attitudes, beliefs, and emotional states), interpersonal

Intrapersonal (self)	Interpersonal (others)	Environmental (the world)
Feeling sad	Criticized by my boss	Smell of a barbecue

(e.g., your relationship with your partner), and environmental (for e.g., family beliefs and attitudes, peer group, and community) triggers that pose the biggest threat to you. It is not important at this stage to be comprehensive in your list; just pick those items which may be the most challenging for your sobriety that first come to mind. We provide an example of each type of trigger to help you get started.

Trigger Map

For this exercise, choose one of your triggers identified in Exercise 2.1 and write it inside the oval on the Map. Imagine yourself being in the situation and then take a couple of minutes to scatter your thoughts and feelings about that situation around the outside of the oval. Don't edit or second-guess, just write down whatever thoughts come to mind. In Exercise 2.2, we provide an example of a completed Map. A blank Map template follows the example.

Example

Trigger Map 1

What if I am going
to get fired?

I should have a thicker
skin with feedback from
others

My boss should be more
interested in what's going
on in my personal life

I will feel
uncomfortable
now whenever I
am around my
boss or co-workers

Criticized by my boss

I shouldn't feel
self-doubt

Anxious and
worried

I don't know how to
stand up for myself

Description of body tension? _Tension in my chest, dry throat_

Trigger Map 1

Description of body tension: _____

When you've finished writing your thoughts, answer these questions at the bottom of the Map: How much body tension am I experiencing? Where in my body do I notice any tension? How do I describe it?

Trigger Map with Sensory Awareness

Now for Map 2 write the same trigger you wrote in the oval of Map 1 in the oval of this Map.

Begin by first getting comfortable in your chair and focusing on what you are currently doing. Next, just sit and listen to the background sounds. As you listen, feel your feet on the floor, the weight of your body on your seat. Feel the fabric of your clothing, the tabletop, or just rub the tips of your fingers together while you continue to listen to the background sounds. If a thought distracts you, return to listening to the background sounds.

Once you begin to feel settled, write around the oval the thoughts and feelings that come to your mind now about the situation. As you write, feel the pen in your hand and watch the ink flow onto the paper while continually focusing on the background sounds. As with the previous Map, don't edit. There are no right or wrong thoughts. Just let your thoughts stream while you are tuned into your senses.

After a couple of minutes, stop writing and at the bottom of Map 2 provide a description of your body tension. Where do you experience it in your body? How do you experience it?

Now, compare Map1 (Exercise 2.2) and Map 2 (Exercise 2.3). In the space in Exercise 2.4 write down a very brief (one or two sentences) description of your experience of doing Map 1 and then do the same for Map 2. The situation in the oval is the same on both Maps, but what is different about your experience of the two Maps? What, if anything, has shifted for you? Write down your thoughts.

Like the previous high-risk situation Map, did you experience more tension in Map 1 than in Map 2? Did you experience less stress and more lightness when completing Map 2? Was there more mental clutter in Map 1 than in Map 2?

Trigger Map 2

Description of body tension: _____

Map 1	Map 2

Difference between Maps:

The trigger did not change, but your orientation toward it probably did. When you did Map 1 you likely attributed all your distress to the trigger itself. But your body tension and mental clutter decreased when you did Map 2, even though the trigger is the same. This exercise demonstrates that there is something else (which you now know is your I-System) besides the trigger that is causing your distress.

Map 1 (Exercise 2.2) helps you see that when your I-System is overactive it makes it more difficult to manage a triggering situation. This is because when you attempt to deal with a trigger or any troubling, stressful, or painful situation in I-System Functioning it limits your awareness and ability to act optimally. When your I-System is active, it hinders your ability to draw on your recovery capital and skills and thereby limits your choices to a few habitual behaviors. And for those struggling with addiction, relapse is often the default response when confronted with triggers or high-risk situations.

In Map 2 (Exercise 2.3) you likely experienced some release from I-System Functioning. When you release this hindrance your capacity to effectively deal with a trigger dramatically increases because you have full access to your recovery capital and skills. You become the larger vessel we referred to earlier.

In Exercise 2.5, we are going to look for the Requirements associated with the triggers that get your I-System going when they are violated.

Go back to Trigger Map 1 and circle the thoughts inside the Map that cause a great deal of mind clutter and body tension. Then ask yourself how you would like each one you circled to be? Sometimes the Requirement is as simple as being the opposite of the thought on the Map, and other times you can identify a Requirement by asking the question "What is my Requirement for this situation?"

Write the thoughts you circled as "should" or "must" statements. Connect each circled thought to its "should" or "must" statement with a line (see example Map (Exercise 2.5): Thought: *I don't know how to stand up for myself*-> Requirement: *I should know how to stand up for myself*). You may have written some of the thoughts on your Map as "should" or "must" statements. If you did, just circle them (see example Map: Thought: *I should have thicker skin with feedback from others*).

As previously mentioned, when you realize that a Requirement has been violated and has triggered your I-System, you are using a Recovery Resilience Practice called Recognize Requirements. As you have learned, it is not only the trigger situation (the "what") that causes your I-System to become active, but rather the Requirements we (often automatically and out of awareness) have regarding that situation. It is often a violated Requirement associated with a trigger situation that makes it more difficult to manage.

Recognizing your Requirements allows you to break free from the box the I-System puts you in and leads to the benefits of Natural Functioning, which permits you to better handle the situation at hand and move forward with your day. When you Recognize Requirements, you will likely experience a shift from I-System Functioning to Natural Functioning.

Example

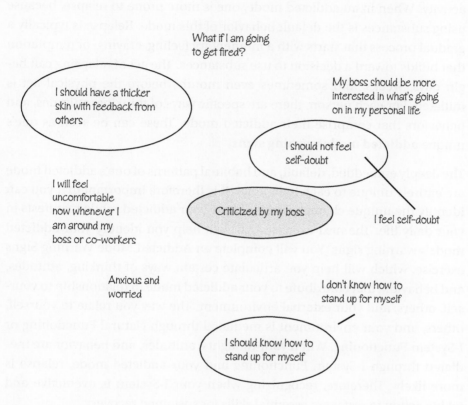

Trigger Map 1

What if I am going
to get fired?

I should have a thicker
skin with feedback from
others

My boss should be more
interested in what's going
on in my personal life

I should not feel
self-doubt

I will feel
uncomfortable
now whenever I
am around my
boss or co-workers

Criticized by my boss

I feel self-doubt

Anxious and
worried

I don't know how to
stand up for myself

I should know how to
stand up for myself

Description of body tension? <u>Tension in my chest, dry throat</u>

Addicted Mode Warning Signs

You have learned that your thinking, attitudes, and behavior can either be driven by Natural Functioning or I-System Functioning. You've also learned that all aspects of your addicted mode are caused or amplified by I-System activity. When in an addicted mode, one is more prone to relapse, because using substances is the default behavior of this mode. Relapse is typically a gradual process that starts with a momentary feeling, craving, or temptation that builds toward a decision to use substances. The act of relapsing can begin days, weeks, and sometimes even months before the physical act is initiated. For each person, there are specific ways of thinking, attitudes, and behaviors that comprise their addicted mode. These can be seen as one's unique **addicted mode warning signs.**

The deeply embedded, default, and habitual patterns of one's addicted mode are entirely unique to each individual. It is therefore important that you can identify the unique characteristics of how your addicted mode manifests in your daily life. The next exercise (2.6) will help you identify your addicted mode's warning signs. You will complete an Addicted Mode Warning Signs exercise, which will help you articulate certain ways of thinking, attitudes, and behaviors that contribute to your addicted mode in relationship to yourself, others, and your external environment. The way you relate to yourself, others, and your environment is mediated through Natural Functioning or I-System Functioning. When your thoughts, attitudes, and behavior are mediated through I-System Functioning and your addicted mode, relapse is more likely. Therefore, recognizing when your I-System is overactive and taking action to rest it are essential skills for sustained recovery.

A common feature of an addicted mode is the habitual, compulsive thinking patterns associated with it. These habitual thinking patterns, often referred to in recovery culture as "stinking thinking," are typically characterized by thoughts and narratives that reinforce and rationalize your substance use. Examples of addictive, "stinking thinking" patterns are denial, rationalization, blame, excessive self-pity, self-obsession, resentment, projection, over-personalization, and other types of defense mechanisms and/or cognitive distortions. When cravings and "stinking thinking" arise, it is crucial that you recognize that they are part of your addicted mode, made possible by your overactive

I-System. Developing this awareness and coupling it with Sensory Awareness will help you shift to a Natural Functioning mode where you will be able to access your recovery capital and employ your recovery skills to cope with the cravings. When you experience a shift from I-System Functioning to Natural Functioning you know you are back on the recovery pathway.

As highlighted in *Figure 2*, there are two potential trajectories when confronted with addicted mode warning signs. One can lead to relapse. The other follows the recovery pathway. At the crossroads is the opportunity to use your Recovery Resilience Practice to shift to Natural Functioning or to not use your practice and potentially slip into addicted mode. The ability to use various recovery skills or otherwise draw on your recovery capital, your recovery resilience, is influenced by whether the I-System or Natural Functioning is in the driver's seat. If the I-System is in control, then thinking and actions may occur within the addicted mode. Conversely, if the I-System is resting, thinking and actions will occur within the Natural Functioning mode. The mode you are in will influence your capacity to effectively apply all your recovery skills and tools.

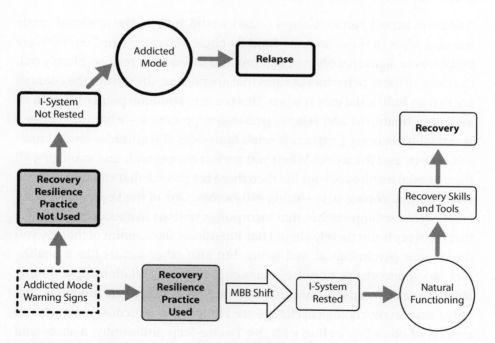

Figure 2 Relapse versus Natural Functioning pathways.

To provide a general overview of how your addicted mode warning signs can manifest, we look at it from three general areas or perspectives: self, others, and the world. (1) *Self:* refers to all aspects of you as an individual, which includes all aspects of your internal world and behavior and would include areas like physical health and behaviors like sleep and diet; your beliefs and thought processes; your emotional life and general psychological well-being; existential, that is, your goals and aspirations, and what you find meaningful, as well as your spiritual/religious beliefs. (2) *Others:* refers to all your interpersonal, social relationships, and cultural influences. (3) *World:* refers to your immediate environment, for example the state of your house, and all your administrative, legal, and monetary dealings, as well as events and situations in the world.[2] We will keep referring to these three areas (self, others, and the world) throughout the workbook, as it provides a simple and fundamental framework for viewing our existence or what existential philosophers refers to as our "being-in-the-world." When our I-Systems are overactive, it distorts the way we think, perceive, and act within and across these dimensions of our lives, causing us to miss or dismiss warning signs when the arise. Conversely, when our I-Systems are rested, we see things, including warning signs, "as they really are."

Addiction expert Patrick Carnes (2008) would refer to the addicted mode warning signs in these areas as "middle circle behavior/signs" as these are behaviors or signs that often or can proceed or lead to a relapse. Simply put, the more of these behaviors or signs that are present, the greater the chances are that an individual may relapse. This is a very common point of view in all addiction treatment and relapse prevention programs – what influences a sustainable recovery program is one's behaviors and attitudes toward oneself, others, and the world. When you are not coping with and managing all the essential features of your life then there is a chance that you will revert to your habitual coping style – using substances. One of the key insights of effective recovery approaches that incorporate notions like recovery capital is that recovery is not merely about your intentions, the amount of therapy you do, or your psychological well-being, but also other factors like a healthy diet, adequate sleep, exercise, managing finances, relationships, finding meaning, etc. Relapse prevention and addiction treatment programs that only focus on psychological change are limited – as addiction permeates all aspects of one's life. In line with the Twelve-Step philosophy, a successful and sustainable recovery program requires a complete lifestyle change.

Using the template on the next page (Exercise 2.6) write down, in the space provided – for self, others, and the world, respectively – which of your thoughts, attitudes, and behaviors normally accompany or precede your substance use and have typically been a part of your addicted mode. In other words, you will identify relapse warning signs in each of these three areas. Try and be as comprehensive as possible. For example, for self: it may be poor sleep hygiene, eating junk food, euphoric recall (of prior intoxicated states), rationalization, thinking about positive aspects of using, dwelling on negative feelings like anger or sadness, attitudes like self-pity or resentment, lack of meaning, and/or hopelessness about the future. In assessing the category of "others" you might identify being socially isolated, not going to your support group, or not reaching out to your support system when going through a difficult time. In assessing the world, it might include being reckless with your spending, your house being untidy, consistently arriving late for work, procrastinating with studies, being upset about politics, etc. We provide an example to help you get started.

What you wrote down in each area can be understood as warning signs, or red flags, which indicate that your thinking, attitudes, or behavior (factors that are in your control) that are associated with and feed your addicted mode are making you more prone to relapse (increasing your disposition toward addictive behavior). The aim of developing a Recovery Resilience Practice is to develop a lifestyle where your daily activities and coping strategies are mediated through Natural Functioning instead of an addicted mode (I-System driven). It is therefore important to understand the "who" that is influencing your thinking, attitudes, and behavior – you in Natural Functioning or you in your addicted mode.

As you develop the ability to notice that you are entering into an addicted mode (noticing addicted mode warning signs) and that your I-System is overactive (by practicing Recognizing I-System Activity), it allows you to do something proactive about it. For example, if/when you have a day where you feel particularly ungrateful with excessive thoughts of self-pity and you recognize that these thoughts are associated with I-System activity and your addicted mode, you can then use your Recovery Resilience Practice (e.g., Mapping, Sensory Awareness) to shift to Natural Functioning. Doing this will allow you to see things more realistically instead of falling victim to your addicted mode and I-System's mirages.

Example

	Addicted Mode Warning Signs
Self	Eating too much sugar Resentful toward my parents Obsessing about the past Did not do any step work this week Feeling hopeless about my life
Others	Isolating Turning down invitations Arguing with partner Poor relationship with coworker
The World	Spent too much money on clothes House untidy Late with taxes Procrastinating with my studies Not paying bills on time

Addicted Mode Warning Signs	
Self	
Others	
The World	

Recovery as a Way of Life

When you incorporate a Recovery Resilience Practice into your daily activities and recovery program, they will not only help prevent relapse and build recovery resilience but also will help you over time to flourish in all aspects of your life. The approach outlined in this workbook is based on the premise (similar to the Twelve-Step philosophy) that addiction is a dysfunctional way of being-in-the-world and that stopping the use of substances is only one aspect of a sustainable recovery process. In short, one needs a complete lifestyle change – a change from a lifestyle dominated by the I-System and the addicted mode to one guided by moment to moment Natural Functioning. Without a change in lifestyle, it is highly likely that the I-System-driven addicted mode will prevail and thereby hinder your ability to use your recovery capital and skills to stay on the recovery pathway. Instead of accessing your coping and self-regulating skills, you may eventually gravitate back to your previous habitual and addictive mode of being-in-the-world.

This change in lifestyle is done "just for today," moment by moment. In the "Big Book" of Alcoholics Anonymous it highlights this notion that recovery is a "way of life"[3] and the necessity of engaging in activities of daily living that are guided by a desire for personal growth:

> AA is not a plan for recovery that can be finished and done with. **It is a way of life**, and the challenge contained in its principles is great enough to keep any human being striving for as long as he lives. We do not, cannot, outgrow this plan ... We must have a program for living that allows for limitless expansion ... However, this isn't as rough as it sounds as we do become grateful for the necessity that makes us toe the line, for we find that we are more than compensated for a consistent effort by the countless dividends we receive. (Wilson, 1979, p. 311)

The notion of recovery as a way of life highlights that a sustainable recovery is a way of being-in-the-world where our basic human needs are met through healthy means in contrast to a lifestyle where our needs are met through substance use and other dysfunctional methods. Simply put, substance use and addiction can be seen as a dysfunctional way of attempting to satisfy basic human needs. To highlight this, we will look at the relationship between substance abuse and altered states of consciousness and preferred styles of coping. Anybody that has used psychoactive substances would agree that it results in an alteration of consciousness, or an altered state of consciousness. In fact, the aim of using psychoactive substances is to enter a certain altered state, and various types of substances create various types of altered states. Some researchers believe that humans have an innate drive to seek altered states of consciousness (Du Plessis, 2018; McPeak et al., 1991; Winkelman, 2001), and that individuals who abuse psychoactive substances follow a normal human motive to achieve altered states of consciousness, but use maladaptive methods because they are not provided with the opportunity to learn "constructive alternative methods for experiencing non-ordinary consciousness" (Winkelman, 2001, p. 340).

From this viewpoint, substance use is then understood as a dysfunctional method to meet a basic human need. Alcoholics Anonymous echoes this view and suggests its participants find "a new state of consciousness and being" to replace the self-destructive pursuit of alcohol-induced altered states of consciousness with a healthier life-enhancing approach (Wilson, 1987, p. 106). Similarly, psychologists Richard Ulman and Harry Paul in their book *The Self Psychology of Addiction: Narcissus in Wonderland* (2006, p. 63) point out the need for individuals in recovery to find healthy means to achieve altered states of consciousness. They state that "[s]uch an altered state of consciousness may eventually supersede and supplant [an individual's] dependence on an addictive state of mind."

Our innate need for altered states of consciousness is also related to how we cope with stress and psychic pain. Feeling good and avoiding unnecessary pain are universal needs. To feel good, we seek out activities that alter our brain chemistry (McCauley, 2010). Addiction can be understood as this normal need gone awry. Addicts have found a dysfunctional way to meet this innate need through substance use or certain behaviors to which they have become addicted. One fascinating line of research has discovered a striking correlation between preferred coping styles and one's drugs of choice. The researchers found that individuals who preferred depressants, like heroin, used passive withdrawal, as well as reduced sensory stimulation, as their primary coping skills (Milkman & Sunderworth, 2010), whereas those who preferred stimulants, like amphetamines, were prone to confront a hostile environment with intellectual or physical activity.

Those who used hallucinogens, like lysergic acid diethylamide (LSD), sought daydreaming and imagery to aid in reducing tension.

Addiction researchers Harvey Milkman and Stanley Sunderworth (2010, p. 19) state that "After studying life histories of drug abusers, we have seen that drugs of choice are harmonious with an individual's usual means of coping with stress." They go on to state that:

> the drug group of choice depressants [satiation], stimulants [arousal], or hallucinogens [fantasy] – is the one that best fits the individual's characteristic way of coping with stress or feelings of unworthiness. People do not become addicted to drugs or mood-altering activities as such, but rather to the satiation, arousal, or fantasy experiences that can be achieved through them. (Milkman & Sunderworth, 2010, p. 19)

Based on the above discussion, it is imperative for individuals in recovery to find healthy activities related to their preferred coping style (satiation, arousal, or fantasy), in light of the research finding that this preferred coping style often correlates with their drug of choice. We assert that Natural Functioning is the state of consciousness and mode of being-in-the-world that sustains recovery whereas I-System Functioning derails it. Thus, the aim of this workbook is for you to develop a Recovery Resilience Practice that leads to moment by moment Natural Functioning wherein you are naturally more creative and thus have more capacity to access healthy ways of coping and find healthy ways to meet your basic human needs. Simply put, in Natural Functioning mode, you have more options and will find more creative ways to take care of yourself and stay on the recovery pathway.

In summary, we have seen that any activity is driven either by I-System Functioning or Natural Functioning. What is of primary importance is not only *what* you are doing, but *who* is doing it – your I-System (addicted mode) or you in Natural Functioning. That is, are your daily activities and how you meet your needs driven by your I-System, or are they guided by Natural Functioning? Asking yourself *"who"* is responding to triggers and cravings when they occur and *"who"* is doing the thinking and perceiving as you engage in your activities of daily living will help you develop a sustainable recovery lifestyle.

Recovery Resilience Journal

Step Ten of the Twelve-Step program suggests that individuals continue to take personal inventory. For many people in Twelve-Step programs and for those working other recovery programs, a personal inventory or daily journal is often one of their core recovery practices. It is easy to see why because it affords one the opportunity to do daily psychological "house cleaning." In Step Ten it is often suggested to look for emotional disturbances and attitudes that can trigger one to return to misusing drugs or alcohol. Watching for these disturbances and attitudes (signs of your addicted mode and overactive I-System) daily – and taking a daily inventory – is an important part of recovery.

Therefore, regularly incorporating awareness of addicted mode warning signs into your daily journaling can be of great benefit. With this awareness comes the power to act. You do not have to be a hostage to your I-System and addicted mode. Remember, the opportunity to experience the Shift is ever present. For this reason, we strongly recommend that you start, if you have not already started, the practice of keeping a daily journal or inventory. We recommend incorporating the Recovery Resilience Journal template as part of your daily inventory. Or, if you have a book that you use as a journal you can do a similar exercise in your book.

In the next exercise (2.7), you will practice completing your daily journal. On the blank Recovery Resilience Journal template, write down how addicted mode warning signs have manifested in these life domains: self, others, and the world. Also, write down the Recovery Resilience Practices you used in these domains. See the example (Exercise 2.7) provided. While developing your Recovery Resilience Practice, it will be useful to use the template. Eventually you can incorporate it into your daily journal or Step Ten daily inventory in a less structured manner. Keep in mind that while the journal is completed at the end of the day, your Recovery Resilience Practice is implemented in each moment of your activities of daily living.

Well done for completing Chapter 2 of the Workbook. Next we provide an overview of the components of a Recovery Resilience Practice introduced thus far.

Example

Recovery Resilience Journal

	Addicted Mode Warning Signs	Recovery Resilience Practice
Self	Eating too much sugar Resentful toward my parents Obsessing about the past	Sensory Awareness Recognize Requirements Experienced the Shift when I Recognized Requirements.
Others	Isolating Arguing with partner Poor relationship with coworker	Mapping Recognized I-System Activity and Experienced the Shift Recognized Requirements
The World	Spent too much money on clothes Procrastinating with my studies Not paying bills on time	Used Sensory Awareness Mapping Asked myself "who" is making these choices? Recognized I-System Activity

Recovery Resilience Journal

	Addicted Mode Warning Signs	Recovery Resilience Practice
Self		
Others		
The World		

OVERVIEW OF CHAPTER 2

Recovery Resilience Practice

- Do **Mapping** related to any high-risk situation, trigger, or troubling experience.
- **Recognize I-System Activity** by being aware of body tension and mind clutter.
- Practice **Sensory Awareness**.
- **Recognize Requirements** when performing daily activities.
- **Experience the Shift.**

On the next few pages please fill out the following:

Addicted Mode Warning Signs: Use the template and write down, in the space provided your addicted mode warning signs for the past week. Try and be as comprehensive as possible.

Flourishing Scale: Complete the scale and calculate and your score, from 1 to 7, for each question over the past week or two.

Recovery Resilience Practice Scale: Complete the scale and calculate and write down the frequency of your Recovery Resilience Practice. Indicate whether it was never, hardly ever, occasionally, or regularly.

We recommend practicing what was outlined in this chapter for 1–2 weeks before moving on to the next chapter.

Addicted Mode Warning Signs

Date: _____

Over the past week write down how your I-System has been active in each of your life dimensions.

	Addicted Mode Warning Signs
Self	
Others	
The World	

Flourishing Scale

Date: _____

Below are eight statements with which you may agree or disagree. Using the 1–7 scale below, indicate your agreement with each item by indicating that response for each statement.

- 7 – Strongly agree
- 6 – Agree
- 5 – Slightly agree
- 4 – Neither agree nor disagree
- 3 – Slightly disagree
- 2 – Disagree
- 1 – Strongly disagree

Indicate your agreement with each item	(1–7)
I lead a purposeful and meaningful life	
My social relationships are supportive and rewarding	
I am engaged and interested in my daily activities	
I actively contribute to the happiness and well-being of others	
I am competent and capable in the activities that are important to me	
I am a good person and live a good life	
I am optimistic about my future	
People respect me	
Total score:	_____

The *Flourishing Scale* was developed by Diener, E., Wirtz, D., Tov, W., et al. (2010). New measures of well-being: Flourishing and positive and negative feelings. *Social Indicators Research*, 39, 247–266.

Recovery Resilience Practice Scale

Date: _____

Over the past week indicate the frequency of your Recovery Resilience Practice. Check the description that most closely reflects your practice: never, hardly ever, or occasionally.

Frequency of Recovery Resilience Practice	Never	Hardly Ever	Occasionally	Regularly
Recognize I-System Activity				
Mapping				
Sensory Awareness				
Recognize Requirements				
Experience the Shift				

3

. . . .

You Can't Fix What's
Not Broken

*I saw that all the things I feared, and which feared me had nothing good
or bad in them save insofar as the mind was affected by them.*
Baruch Spinoza, *Works of Spinoza Vol. II*

There is a strong link between the capacity to cope with negative emotional
states and substance abuse (Baumeister, 2001). As already discussed in the
Introduction, it has been proposed that substance use may be a form of
self-medication that individuals use to cope with their painful and unstable
inner worlds (Khantzian, 1999). Philip Flores (1997, p. 233) believes that addiction can be

> viewed as a misguided attempt at self-repair. Because of unmet develop-
> mental needs, certain individuals will be left with an injured, enfeebled,
> uncohesive, or fragmented self … alcohol, drugs, and other external sources
> of gratification (i.e., food, sex, work, etc.) take on a regulating function while
> creating a false sense of autonomy, independence, and denial of need for
> others.

When individuals use substances as a coping mechanism, this strategy may be
effective in the short term but often proves maladaptive in the long run. The use
of alcohol and drugs provides both negative reinforcement (namely, the reduction of painful feelings via self-medication) and positive reinforcement (that is,

the pleasant experience of being high via positive outcome expectancies). The self-medication hypothesis applies when the individual is using a substance to cope with negative emotions, conflict, or stress (negative reinforcement). From a positive outcome expectancy perspective, the person is focusing on the positive aspects and euphoria of using a substance (positive reinforcement), while ignoring the negative consequences (Brown et al., 1985).

Therefore, an essential component of recovery is learning healthy ways to self-regulate and cope with stress and painful emotions, and the negative thoughts and rumination associated with them. Without healthy coping skills, a key component of recovery capital, individuals in recovery will continue to seek dysfunctional ways of coping and self-regulation (Levin, 1995; Winhall, 2021).

Distressing emotional states can be a by-product of I-System Functioning. In the previous chapters of this workbook, you learned that your Requirements, which are mental rules you have about how you, others, and the world should be, are what activate your I-System when they are violated. You also learned that mental clutter and body tension are signals alerting you that you have drifted off your Natural Functioning course. In the next section (Depressor Map), you will learn about a particularly destructive form of mental clutter that we are all too familiar with – intrusive negative thoughts and rumination (repetitive thinking or dwelling on negative feelings).

Negative thinking and rumination are a central feature of the addictive mode. In the next exercise, you will learn about one of the subsystems of the I-System that often lies at the core of your negative thinking and rumination.

Depressor Map

For Exercise 3.1 write the words "Depressor" inside the oval on the Map template provided on the page after the example Map. Around the oval, write down all the negative thoughts you've had about yourself, thoughts you've had when you were feeling down and being self-critical (e.g., *I am lazy, I will never amount to anything*). Don't edit or second-guess, just write down whatever thoughts come to mind.

Example

Depressor Map

I will never be able
to stay clean

I fail at
everything I do

I am a loser

Depressor

I'll never amount
to anything

I am socially
awkward

I don't have what it
takes to stay in
recovery

I am stupid

I am just a bad person

Depressor Map

Look at the thoughts on your Map. Each of them is just a Natural Functioning thought that happens to be negative. Some of these thoughts may create a little distress and some may create a huge amount of distress. However, the problem is not with your negative thoughts but with the activity of the **Depressor**, which according to the I-System Model is a subsystem of your I-System. Depressor activity spins storylines about negative thoughts, keeping you in a cycle of rumination.

Negative and self-critical thoughts come and go. What is problematic is when we are caught in a cycle of rumination about these thoughts. We will investigate this more in the next section (Depressor Storylines).

Depressor Storylines

In the space provided in Exercise 3.2, take one of the negative thoughts from your Depressor Map that has the most associated body tension and write down the story associated with that thought. We provide an example to help you to see how to do this.

What you have written down, whether it consisted of a couple of thoughts or a lengthier story, is called a **Depressor Storyline**. Depressor Storylines are generally about not being "good enough" and being "damaged" (various feelings and sensations of embarrassment, humiliation, shame, and self-loathing such as "*I will never amount to anything*"). Depressor Storylines can also be about others and your environment or the world (e.g., storylines associated with "*People cannot be trusted*"). Depressor Storylines may play out in your mind many times throughout the day, cluttering your mind, and creating mental lapses, errors, misperceptions, misjudgments, and/or procrastination.

I-System Functioning and your addicted mode are sustained by Depressor Storylines. For sustained and successful addiction recovery, it is crucial to be aware of Depressor Storylines. The negativity you experience when these types of storylines are playing in your mind is often a contributing factor in relapse (Marlatt & Gordon, 1980; Winhall, 2021). Below are some common thoughts that may have accompanied your Depressor Storylines:

- *I am a failure at everything I do.*
- *I don't think I can handle life without using.*

Thought: I am a loser.

Story: Every time I try to do anything I screw it up. People must think I'm useless. I'll never get things right. Why should I care or try?

_____

_____

_____

_____

_____

_____

_____

_____

_____

_____

_____

_____

_____

_____

_____

_____

_____

_____

- *Life won't be fun – I won't be fun – without using.*
- *I'm worried I will turn into someone I don't like.*
- *I am boring sober.*
- *My cravings will be overwhelming; I won't be able to resist them.*
- *If I stop, I'll only start up again; I have never finished anything.*
- *I'm worried that I have been so damaged by my addiction that I won't be able to recover.*
- *People cannot be trusted.*
- *Life is unfair.*

What triggers your Depressor to generate these storylines? It is a violated Requirement. For example, you may have a Requirement that *"I should be successful,"* and when you fail at something, your Depressor starts to spin storylines around the thought *"I am a failure at everything I do."* Whenever a Requirement is violated, it always activates the Depressor.

For example, go back to the *"How I Would Like to Be"* Map in Chapter 1 (Exercise 1.5) and focus on how you felt when your Requirement for yourself was violated (e.g., if the item inside the circle was *"I should be successful,"* you confirmed it was a Requirement by the body tension and negative emotional response associated with the opposite item outside the circle, i.e., experiencing yourself as a failure). The negative emotions and body tension you experienced were amplified by your Depressor.

Remember, the purpose of your Requirements is to support a certain self-image and identity. The Requirements you identified like *"I should be strong"* are intended to support this self-image. These Requirements are the fabric or glue that holds together a mental picture or self-schema of who you think you are. Self-schemas are stable and often rigid beliefs about oneself and one's relationship with others and the world. Basically, these schemas form the glasses through which we look at the world.

The problem is that your I-System can construct an overly rigid and limited mental picture of who you think you are through the generation of Requirements. When these Requirements are violated, your Depressor starts to generate negative storylines associated with the violated Requirement. Simply put, your Requirements support a certain self-image or mental picture of who you think you are and when this is threatened by the violation of a Requirement, it results in the generation of Depressor Storylines. These Depressor Storylines are usually accompanied by very painful emotional states and, consequently, there is often the desire to medicate or counteract these painful feelings.

Depressor Storylines Fuel Your Addicted Mode

Now we will look more in-depth at how Depressor Storylines can fuel your addicted mode.

Requirement	What violates the Requirement?
My partner should not argue with me	My partner argues with me
I should not feel so sad	When I feel sad
Life should be fair	An earthquake that killed thousands of people

In Exercise 3.3, write down three Requirements that underlie high-risk situations or triggers related to yourself, others, and the world, and which normally elicit a strong negative emotional response. For example, "*My partner should not argue with me.*" Then opposite it, write down a situation or event (internal or external) that would violate the particular Requirement (e.g., *My partner argues with me*). We provide a few examples to show you how to do this.

Now choose one of the situations or events from the above "What Violates the Requirement?" list and in the space provided in Exercise 3.4, write down a negative story you tell yourself when that situation happens. There is no right or wrong answer; it does not matter how irrational your thoughts or stories may be. Simply try to be as honest as you can and write down your thoughts in the form of a story without editing. It is not important to be comprehensive, just try to write down the essence of the story. Again, we provide an example to help you see how to do this.

Situation: I feel sad and have a Requirement that I should not feel so sad.

Story: I seem to always feel sad. I don't think I'll ever not feel sad again. It seems like the only time I don't feel sad is when I'm using. I'll never figure this out. Why can't I just be happy? What's wrong with me?

_____

_____

_____

_____

_____

_____

_____

_____

_____

_____

_____

_____

_____

Depressor Storylines are a core aspect of your addiction mode and the toxic shame that accompany it. Simply put, the Depressor makes an unpleasant situation or disappointment far more unbearable by creating a narrative that makes you feel ashamed and not good enough as a human being, or excessively disappointed in others and the world. There are many things we are not good at, and sometimes we make mistakes, which lead to healthy feelings of disappointment, guilt, and a desire to improve. But the feelings of self-loathing and thoughts that we are just not good enough as human beings are Depressor-driven, self-shaming I-System fictions. When these narratives clutter your mind, your ability to draw on your recovery capital is severely compromised. And, perhaps most destructive of all is their impact on your self-image. If you tell yourself these stories long enough, they come to falsely define who you think you are.

In the next section (The Depressor and the Abstinence Violation Effect), we will look at the role the Depressor plays in relapse.

The Depressor and the Abstinence Violation Effect

The thoughts and feelings of Depressor-driven toxic shame often precede and follow a lapse or relapse. A lapse can be understood as a onetime, typically brief episode of drinking or using substances, whereas a relapse represents a total immersion back into an addicted lifestyle. The Depressor is very active after either a lapse or relapse and therefore tills the soil for future relapse. It becomes a vicious cycle, where after each relapse there are more powerful Depressor Storylines, which in turn make you more prone to subsequent relapse. "I used to drink," writes John Bradshaw (1988, p. 36) "to solve the problems caused by drinking. The more I drank to relieve my shame-based loneliness and hurt, the more I felt ashamed."

In the context of the relapse process, the Depressor contributes to what is called the "abstinence violation effect," which is the self-blame, guilt, shame, and loss of perceived control that individuals often experience after the violation of self-imposed rules (Curry et al., 1987). An individual may have the Depressor Storyline that *"Now that I have failed and lost my clean time, I might as well just keep on using"* or *"I am such a loser that I will never be able to stay clean for long."* A person may experience the abstinence violation effect when after some clean time he/she experiences a lapse; for example, there may be feelings of guilt, shame, and hopelessness. This is often triggered by the discrepancy between one's present lapse into addictive behavior and one's prior identity as an abstainer. The thoughts associated with the abstinence violation effect are more likely to progress to relapse if an individual views a lapse as an irreparable failure (Miller et al., 1996). However, if the same individual interprets the lapse as a transitional learning experience, then the progression to relapse or full-blown addiction is far less likely (Curry et al., 1987). Those individuals who perceive a lapse as a learning experience will be more likely to use alternative coping strategies in the future which may lead to more effective responses in high-risk situations (i.e., increased recovery capital).

In fact, the authors can vouch, based on their experience of working in various inpatient and outpatient programs, for the palpable difference in outcomes between those who view relapse as a failure (often as the result of

Depressor Storylines) versus those that see relapse as a learning opportunity (a Natural Functioning orientation). Not infrequently, for example, when a client returns to treatment after discharge, often directly in the wake of relapse, they are encouraged and supported to share their relapse experience – including events leading up to it – with the rest of the treatment center group. This way, all group members can benefit and contribute useful strategies for moving forward. And most importantly, the individual that experienced the relapse is not only not shamed by others but is actually seen as providing valuable learning "grist for the mill." Suffice it to say, the whole treatment milieu becomes one of supportive facilitation rather than shame or being otherwise ostracized.

Contrarily, the I-System's Depressor will take the natural feelings of disappointment after a lapse or relapse and spin them into a storyline of unbearable thoughts and feelings of disappointment and shame. This fuels one's addicted mode, making continued use more likely in the immediate future. This is important to remember as you may experience a lapse or relapse at various stages of your recovery journey.

In Exercise 3.5, recall the negative self-talk or Depressor Storylines that you experienced with past lapses or relapses. Think of those times when you did not want to use but did, and how you felt afterward. In this exercise it is not important to be comprehensive, just write down the essence of the story.

Learning how to recognize Depressor activity is imperative to prevent a lapse or to effectively recover from a lapse or relapse. Recognizing these storylines allows you to defuse them in real time, as they happen. You will learn how to do this. But first, we will explore how Depressor activity contributes to toxic shame.

The Depressor and Toxic Shame

John Bradshaw, author of *Healing the Shame that Binds You,* argues that toxic shame is often the motivator behind addictive behaviors (as well as many other dysfunctional behaviors). Bradshaw makes the distinction between healthy shame and toxic shame. Healthy shame lets us know that to be human

I'm a hopeless addict. I've ruined my life. I'll never get this right. What's the point of trying?

_____
_____
_____
_____
_____
_____
_____
_____
_____
_____
_____
_____
_____
_____
_____
_____
_____
_____

is to be limited and provides us with a healthy sense of humility. Healthy shame is an emotion that teaches us about our limits and, like all emotions, it moves us to get our basic human needs met. On the other hand, toxic shame is a deep-seated belief that we are fundamentally flawed and simply not good enough as human beings. As Friedrich Nietzsche stated, "Everyone needs a sense of shame, but no one needs to feel ashamed" (in Bradshaw, 1988, p. 1).

A shame-based belief system is essentially composed of negative thoughts and storylines about being fundamentally flawed, and not good enough, and that you need to be fixed. When the Depressor is active it replays these stories and generates additional stories about not being good enough. Individuals often abuse substances in a futile effort to repair the illusion that they are not good enough and to numb the painful and often overwhelming feelings associated with toxic shame. As Bradshaw highlights, "This deep internalized shame gives rise to distorted thinking. The distorted thinking can be reduced to the belief that I'll be okay if I drink, eat, have sex, get more money, work harder, etc." (Bradshaw, 1988, p. 1).

It is impossible to rid yourself completely of negative thoughts and it wouldn't necessarily be advisable to do so even if you could. Some negative thoughts play an important regulatory role psychologically, for example, when you have negative thoughts associated with guilt. Toxic shame is tied to the idea that it is *you* that is fundamentally "bad" or "broken" rather than the behaviors you sometimes engage in. It is often the Depressor that amplifies these shame-based thoughts. Toxic shame is an example of when negative thoughts become problematic due to I-System overactivity; when they lead to "broken record" rumination and/or chronic discomfort in your body. If you don't recognize them for what they are, you can come to believe that "this is just who I am." This fictitious view of yourself limits your choices to only those that are congruent with it. The fiction that is common with addicted populations, the shame-based belief of being "damaged and not good enough," will by default hinder resilience and limit an individual's capacity to find creative ways of dealing with adversity.

Fortunately, you can learn how to stop the Depressor from spinning all these stories about yourself, others, and the world. You cannot do much about negative thoughts that arise in the moment, but you can control how the Depressor amplifies these negative thoughts. This will be the focus of our next section (Defuse Depressor Storylines).

Defuse Depressor Storylines

Recall that lacking adequate coping skills to deal with negative emotional states as well as distressful situations are two strong predictors of drug use and possible relapse when in recovery from addiction. Therefore, understanding and knowing how to deal with the negative thoughts, feelings, and body sensations associated with Depressor activity is imperative for sustained recovery. The good news is that you can develop these crucial skills.

Once your I-System is activated, due to a violated Requirement, your Depressor starts to spin Depressor Storylines about the situation, which clouds the moment with negativity. The Depressor activity impairs your ability to take care of yourself and your responsibilities. When you realize your Depressor has spun storylines about a negative thought after one of your Requirements was violated, you can use a Recovery Resilience Practice called **Defuse Depressor Storylines**. This can be done by recognizing when the Depressor has spun a storyline about a negative thought and then labeling the thoughts of the Storyline by saying to yourself "I'm having the thought that _____." Repeat this slowly several times and note what happens. You may even add "It's just a thought" or "So what else is new." Try listening to background sounds as you label your thoughts. You will see how labeling a Depressor Storyline allows you to see the truth, which is that a thought is just a thought and that you are not who these thoughts portray you to be.

By labeling your Depressor Storylines, you don't ignore or neglect their content, you are just stopping the Depressor from generating more storylines that keep the I-System active and fuel your addicted mode, leaving you at far greater risk of relapse.

It is important to realize the power that Depressor Storylines have on your mind and body each moment. Without recognizing your Depressor's activities, it is very difficult, or even impossible, to see things as they really are. Shining your light of awareness on and interrupting these storylines helps you access your Natural Functioning. Recognizing and defusing these storylines will help you experience the shift from a I-System mode or addicted mode to a Natural Functioning mode.

As we have mentioned, the arena of your practice is your activities of daily living. The aim of your Recovery Resilience Practice is to improve how you live your life and help you stay on the recovery pathway. As we have highlighted, your I-System is like a compass and provides a signal when you are off course. Let's look at some examples of how recognizing and defusing Depressor activity could play out in the context of everyday situations and how you can apply your Recovery Resilience Practice throughout the day.

Example

Situation: Waking up in the morning and experiencing dread and a sinking stomach.

Signal of My Depressor: Sinking stomach and negative self-talk. Negative stories about the future occupy my mind.

Impact of Depressor Activity: Starting the day burdened with intrusive negative thoughts and storylines.

Benefit of Defusing Depressor Storylines: You label your intrusive thoughts and storylines while engaging in Sensory Awareness and start the day with a better attitude.

Example

Situation: Experiencing a craving while eating breakfast when a certain song plays on the radio which causes a racing heart.

Signal of My Depressor: Racing heart and negative thoughts and storylines.

Impact of Depressor Activity: Continue the morning craving and being distracted.

Benefit of Defusing Depressor Storylines: You realize your I-System is overactive, you label your "craving thoughts," experience the Shift and continue the morning mindful of finishing breakfast and completing other tasks to get you ready for the workday.

Example

Situation: Getting a text inviting you to a party that night.

Signal of My Depressor: Troubling thoughts about wanting to go to the party. Telling yourself stories about being a failure at recovery because you want to go to the party.

Impact of Depressor Activity: Carrying negative thoughts and storylines into the evening.

Benefits of Defusing Depressor Storylines: You label your troubling thoughts and storylines, and continue the night with Natural Functioning and enjoy the evening.

For this exercise you will Defuse Depressor Storylines. List the Depressor Storylines from the previous exercise (3.5) and then "thought label" these storylines. We provide an example to help you see how to do this. This exercise may seem unnecessary but doing this will help you to use this practice in real time.

Depressor Storyline: I seem to always feel sad. I don't think I'll ever not feel sad again. It seems like the only time I don't feel sad is when I'm using. I'll never figure this out.

Defuse Depressor Storyline: I'm having the thought that I seem to always feel sad and that I'll always feel sad. So, what else is new?

_____

_____

_____

_____

_____

_____

_____

_____

_____

_____

_____

_____

_____

_____

What differentiates Natural Functioning negative self-talk (which is a normal and unavoidable aspect of human existence) from Depressor negative self-talk is the disproportionate intensity of the unpleasant and painful thoughts, feelings, and body sensations that accompany it. Negative thoughts that are part of Natural Functioning come and go. We don't overidentify with them. They don't clutter our minds or fill our bodies with tension. When we overidentify with them the shame-based feelings caused by the Depressor are often unbearable, and you cannot simply sit with them for extended periods of time. This results in an overbearing feeling or desire to do something about it – a compulsive need to fix the unpleasant and painful shame-based mind-body state caused by your Depressor's activities.

This compulsive need and desire to fix the unpleasant and shamed-based mind-body states caused by the Depressor will be our next topic of discussion.

How I Am Going to Improve My Life

For the next exercise (3.7), using the Map template provided, write around the oval your thoughts about how you are going to improve your life. Don't edit or second-guess, just write down whatever thoughts come to mind. On the next page (Exercise 3.7), we provide an example of a completed Map.

Contemplate each item on the Map and for each of them rate (on a scale from 1 to 3) the amount of body tension you experience as you think about trying to reach your self-improvement goal.

What was the difference in energy you experienced when doing this Map compared to your previous Depressor Map? Do you feel more energized by this Map? What is the difference in body tension? All these thoughts may be natural and normal plans you have about how you are going to improve your life. But when they arise as a result of Depressor activity they take on a different function. We are going to explore this in the next exercise (3.8).

For this exercise (3.8), you will go back to your Depressor Map (Exercise 3.1) at the beginning of this chapter and write down what you feel you need to do about the negative thoughts on the Map. It is normal when experiencing the negativity and shame associated with Depressor Storylines to try and do something about them because it is difficult and even unbearable coping with this type of negativity for very long.

Look at the thoughts on your Depressor Map and write down next to each of them what you feel driven to do about the thought. An example Map is provided (Exercise 3.8).

Example

How I Am Going to Improve My Life Map

I am stopping
drinking

Save money

Go to the gym

Try harder

How I Am Going to
Improve My Life

Loose weight

Find a romantic
partner

Get a degree

How I Am Going to Improve My Life Map

How I am Going to Improve My Life

Example

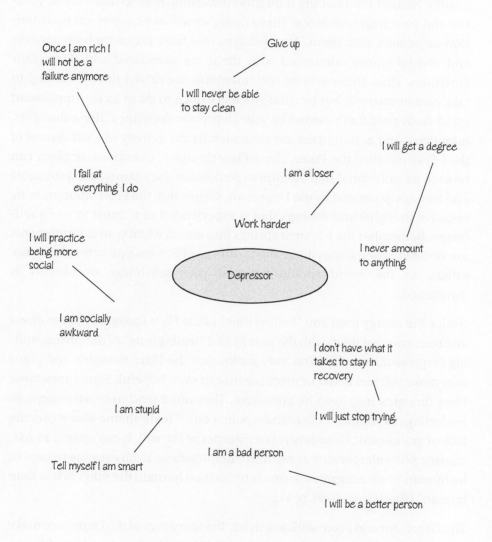

Depressor/Fixer Map

Once I am rich I will not be a failure anymore

Give up

I will never be able to stay clean

I will get a degree

I fail at everything I do

I am a loser

I never amount to anything

Work harder

I will practice being more social

Depressor

I am socially awkward

I don't have what it takes to stay in recovery

I am stupid

I will just stop trying

Tell myself I am smart

I am a bad person

I will be a better person

As highlighted previously, when your Depressor is active you are often overcome by an overwhelming desire to do something to rectify unpleasant feelings or state caused by your Depressor's activities.

Some of what you feel driven to do about your Depressor Storylines may be healthy Natural Functioning thoughts concerning how to take care of yourself and your responsibilities. These thoughts will not have much body tension associated with them. Any thoughts that have excessive body tension and mental clutter connected with them are associated with Depressor Storylines. Thus, these actions and intentions are driven not by wanting to take care of yourself, but by what you feel driven to do to fix the unpleasant mind-body state that's caused by your Depressor Storylines. These thoughts, intentions, and action plans are generated by the activity of a subsystem of the I-System called the **Fixer**. These Fixer thoughts, intentions, or plans can be seen as "solutions" that attempt to counteract the shame-based thoughts and feelings generated by the Depressor. Simply put, the Fixer attempts to fix negative thoughts and feelings that is experienced as a threat to one's self-image. Remember the I-System springs into action when your Requirements are violated, when things don't align with your I-System's picture of how you, others, or the world should be, and your self-image or identity is threatened.

Notice the energy level and "feeling tone" of the Fixer thoughts written down and then contrast them with the energy and "feeling tone" of the corresponding Depressor thoughts. You may notice that the Fixer thoughts and plans may make you feel better or more positive or even hopeful. Sometimes these Fixer thoughts may even be grandiose. They often tend to overcompensate for feelings of shame. As Bradshaw points out: "Toxic shame also wears the face of grandiosity. Grandiosity is a disorder of the will. It can appear as narcissistic self-enlargement or wormlike helplessness. Each extreme refuses to be human. Each exaggerates: one is more than human; the other is less than human" (Bradshaw, 1988, p. 41).

The Depressor and Fixer work as a dyad. The Storylines of the Depressor make you believe that you (or others or the world) are damaged and need fixing. The Fixer is the Depressor's partner that drives overactive, never-ending thoughts, plans, fantasies, and stories about how to fix yourself, others, and the world. In other words, the job of the Fixer is primarily to fix the unpleasant feelings of shame, self-loathing, and of being fundamentally flawed, caused by the Depressor. Depressor activity creates feelings of shame and unworthiness that are so unbearable that you absolutely must do something to get rid of them (e.g., use substances). The Fixer tries to fix the painful state that Depressor activity creates with plans and often euphoria-producing fantasies. It is a normal aspect of our human nature to have a strong impulse to try to remedy painful and unpleasant feelings, but when this impulse is driven by your Fixer it either makes things worse or attempts to create temporary relief, the latter of which unfortunately often leads to negative consequences in the long run. Even though Fixer thoughts and fantasies may consist of various "good" feelings and sensations (e.g., euphoria, ecstasy, elation, and exhilaration), the Depressor is ever-present and ready to remind you that, despite these "good" feelings, you are still not good enough. We refer to this as the Depressor-Fixer Cycle.

All the energy you spend on the Depressor-Fixer Cycle is for naught. The Fixer's plan to repair the feelings of shame, of being broken, and not being worthwhile is based on a Depressor fiction. You cannot fix what is not broken. Therefore, another problem associated with the Fixer is that it will perpetually try and fix something it cannot. And as stated in the Introduction to this workbook, this will keep you, like Sisyphus, trapped in an endless cycle of trying to fix what is not broken.

From the Recovery Resilience Program perspective, substance use or any addictive behavior is often an attempt to "fix" the feelings of pain and shame associated with Depressor Storylines. Addictive behavior is Fixer-driven. You can easily see why it is in fact no coincidence that using drugs is often referred to as getting a "fix."

In summary, the Fixer is the Depressor's faithful partner that drives you in unhealthy and unbalanced ways to repair the painful shame-based state that the Depressor has caused or amplified. The Fixer is energized by the false belief (caused by the Depressor) that you are damaged or not good enough, then tries to fix you. A central feature of the addicted mode is that as your addiction progresses your choices become limited to certain predictable and habitual Fixer-driven behaviors, over which you feel more and more powerless.

The Fixer not only drives addictive behavior but also many of our daily actions and future goals. One way to recognize if a past behavior was Fixer-driven is to notice whether, when it was achieved, you experienced peace of mind and a sense of well-being and accomplishment. If the answer is a resounding "No," then it was very likely Fixer-driven. Why, because regardless of your accomplishments the Depressor just spins another story about how you are still not good enough – and this creates an endless cycle.

Fixer Storylines

In the following exercise (3.9), choose one of your Depressor Storylines from the previous exercise and write down in the space below the thoughts or stories you tell yourself about how you are going to fix what your Depressor tells you is damaged or not good enough. These thoughts or stories can consist of a couple of ideas or can be an elaborate plan or fantasy. In this exercise it is not important to be comprehensive; just try and write down the essence of the story.

EXERCISE 3.9

Depressor storyline: I fail at everything I do.

Fixer Storyline: I will work harder and longer and make more money to prove to myself and others that I am not a failure.

_____

_____

_____

_____

_____

_____

_____

_____

_____

_____

_____

What you have written is called a **Fixer Storyline**. The Fixer creates never-ending stories, and fantasies about how to fix the unpleasant and painful thoughts, feelings, and body sensations created by Depressor activity. While on the surface some of these Fixer Storylines seem helpful, in reality they are counterproductive because they are driven by a misguided intention, that is, to fix feelings of shame created by the Depressor. Fixer Storylines are elaborate "schemas" and "action plans" regarding how this "fixing" or "damage repair" will happen (e.g., "I am going to get straight As," "I am going to lose weight"). Fixer-driven behavior is the implementation of these schemas or plans to try to live according to our Requirements so we can feel comfortable inside our skin once again. Put another way, these so-called solutions are just an attempt to make your Requirements come true. These "solutions" are often short-lived because they are trying to fix something that does not need fixing. For example, wanting and striving to get physically fit is perfectly fine, but if it is an attempt to "fix" feelings of shame, then it is misguided because no amount of physical fitness will resolve deep-seated feelings of shame. In the same way no amount of drug use can resolve the Depressor's shame-based beliefs.

Some fantasies and goals of achieving power, wealth, fame, and success may be entirely Fixer-driven. In these situations, these goals are simply shame-based manifestations of proving to ourselves and others that we are good enough. The problem with Fixer-driven goals is that no matter how successful we are the Depressor is always there to remind us that we are still not good enough after achieving the goals. When we are trapped by a Fixer-driven goal, the only two outcomes are: being successful and not feeling good enough; or being unsuccessful and not feeling good enough. The former represents, at best, a hollow victory, the latter, only defeat.

Moreover, the Fixer is very goal-oriented; all that matters is success or failure. Whereas in Natural Functioning, while success and failure are important, one is also able to enjoy the process of striving toward the goal. Apply this, for example, in the context of a lapse or relapse. Recovery as a process implies that any temporary setback may serve as useful feedback for moving forward, whereas when recovery goals are Fixer-driven there is no allowance for setbacks or "failures," including lapses or relapses. When goals and behaviors are Fixer-driven, it is usually an "all or nothing" proposition.

The Fixer Fuels Your Addictive Behavior

For Exercise 3.10, list three high-risk situations or triggers that have caused or may cause cravings and that may pose a risk for relapse. Then write down your Requirements related to the situation. Then next to each Requirement write down "What violates the Requirement." Next, write down a Depressor Storyline (a short, edited version) that is associated with the violated Requirement. Finally, write down what you feel driven to do (or not do) about the situation or event (Fixer Storyline). We provide three examples.

All of the actions or intentions in the "What Do I Feel Driven to Do About It?" section could be healthy thoughts about how to take care of yourself and your responsibilities. However, in this exercise, when they are the result of your Depressor activity, these actions and intentions are driven not by wanting to take care of yourself, but by what you feel driven to do to fix the unpleasant mind-body state that's caused by Depressor Storylines. Some of the "What Do I Feel Driven to Do About It?" may involve the use of substances, but others can fuel your addicted mode and keep you in a cycle of addiction (e.g., isolating or watching too much TV).

What this exercise (3.10) illustrates is the cycle that the Depressor and Fixer keep you in can fuel your addicted mode and increases the risk for relapse. From the Recovery Resilience Program perspective, substance use (or any addictive behavior) is often an attempt to "fix" the feelings of pain and shame associated with the Storylines the Depressor creates. This sentiment is echoed in the following quote, "Addiction has been described as the belief that whenever there is 'something wrong with me,' it can be 'fixed' by something outside of me … It is no wonder, then, that 'locating divinity in drugs' becomes a kind of spiritual death" (Kurtz & Ketcham, 2002, p. 120).

From a substance use perspective, Fixer Storylines often drive outcome expectancies related to substance use, which are the anticipated effects the individual expects when consuming a mind-altering substance (Jones et al., 2001). However, the individual's drug use outcome expectancies may not necessarily correspond with the actual effects experienced after consumption. For example, an individual may expect to feel more relaxed, happier, and social after using a drug, but the person's actual experience may also include increased tension, sadness, and regret. Research conducted on treatment outcomes has

High-risk/ trigger	Requirement	What violates the Requirement?	Depressor Storyline	What do I feel driven to do about it? (Fixer Storyline)
My partner arguing with me	My partner should not argue with me	My partner argues with me	I am useless in relationships	Give up hope on our relationship ever working; in fact, maybe I should just break up now
Feeling sad	I should not feel so sad	When I feel sad	I am just a loser in whatever I try	Go to the bar for a drink
Dwelling on unfairness in the world	Life should be fair	An earthquake that killed thousands of people	I am too sensitive to live in a world where bad things happen to good people	Smoke a joint and binge-watch TV programs

shown that positive outcome expectancies (often Fixer Storylines) related to drug use are associated with poorer treatment outcomes (Connors et al., 1993) and negative outcome expectancies related to drug use are related to improved treatment outcomes (Jones & McMahon, 1996).

Simply put, overly positive and often unrealistic expectations driven by the Fixer may motivate individuals to use substances, while negative expectations (often much more realistic when viewed in Natural Functioning and framed within the context of the consequences substance use may have) may keep individuals from drinking or using. One reason for this is that when we are in an addicted mode our focus is on immediate reward, and in this limited and contracted state of awareness (I-System Functioning) we don't always have ready access to past experiences and insight into possible consequences or our recovery capital. When this happens, we fail to see things as they really are, thus using can seem like a rational and good idea.

Defuse Fixer Storylines

As we have discussed, from a Recovery Resilience Program perspective, every activity we engage in is either driven by our Fixer or inspired by Natural Functioning. The Depressor works to make you believe that you are damaged or broken and need fixing. But the truth is you are not broken or damaged and you don't need fixing, because in Natural Functioning – who you really are – you are good enough. The activity of your Depressor leads to Fixer Storylines that focus on what you feel you absolutely must do to get rid of the unpleasant and painful thoughts, feelings, and body sensations associated with Depressor Storylines. Fixer Storylines then drive behavior that is not optimal for the imperative of moment (e.g., substance use).

When you realize your Depressor has generated storylines and your Fixer is generating storylines about how to fix the unpleasantness caused by your Depressor activity, you can use a Recovery Resilience Practice called **Defuse Fixer Storylines**. This is done by labeling the thoughts associated with the Fixer Storyline. Merely bringing awareness to your Fixer Storylines will help to break the cycle that your Depressor and Fixer keep you locked in. When labeling your Fixer Storylines, you don't ignore or neglect the content of the thoughts, you are just stopping the Fixer from generating additional stories that keep the I-System active, which fuels your addicted mode and increases your risk of relapse.

If an action is being driven by the Fixer, no matter how hard you try, nothing you do will ever be good enough because the Depressor is still there to disapprove or raise the bar. Fixer behavior/activity will never provide an adequate solution to Depressor Storylines no matter how hard you work at it. Therefore, learning to Defuse Fixer Storylines in action is critical to your recovery resilience and well-being. Below is a list of common signs that you have **Fixer activity**:

- Cravings to use (with limited or no awareness of past damage of substance use)
- Trying to meet Requirements at all costs (e.g., at the cost of relationships, your physical and mental health) Note that it is the ordinary Requirements we encounter every day that often do the most damage
- Excess mental pressure or urgency
- Sense of being excessively driven
- Over-preparation and perfectionism
- Excessive controlling behavior
- Mental obsession
- No sense of satisfaction, well-being, or peace of mind with accomplishment.

To practice how to Defuse Fixer Storylines, list the Fixer Storylines from the previous exercise (3.10) and then "thought label" them. This may seem unnecessary but doing this will help you to Defuse Fixer Storylines when they happen in real time. As usual, we provide an example.

The Fixer and Fundamental Human Needs

Chilean economist Manfred Max-Neef, who developed a theory of fundamental human needs, asserted that we have innate fundamental human needs which we all strive to fulfill, and that an individual's quality of life is correlated with the actualization of these needs. According to Max-Neef any

Fixer Storyline: I will work harder and longer and make more money to prove to myself and others that I am not a failure.

Defuse Fixer Storyline: I'm having the thought that I will work harder and longer and make more money to prove to myself and others that I am not a failure. So what else is new?

_____

_____

_____

_____

_____

_____

_____

_____

_____

_____

_____

_____

_____

"fundamental human need not adequately satisfied generates a pathology" (Max-Neef et al., 1991, p. 22). We all have various ways or methods of satisfying our basic human needs. These methods he calls "satisfiers" (satisfying the need), and various types of "satisfiers" are proposed: violators or destroyers, pseudo-satisfiers, inhibiting satisfiers, singular satisfiers, and synergic satisfiers.

Violators or destroyers are paradoxical in nature because when they are applied to satisfy a need, "not only do they annihilate the possibility of its satisfaction over time, but they also impair the adequate satisfaction of other needs" (Max-Neef et al., 1991, p. 31). Pseudo-satisfiers "generate a false sense of satisfaction of a given need. Although not endowed with the aggressiveness of violators or destroyers, they may on occasion annul, in the not too long term, the possibility of satisfying the need they were originally aimed at fulfilling" (Max-Neef et al., 1991, p. 31). Inhibiting satisfiers tend to over-satisfy a given need, consequently limiting the possibility of other needs being satisfied. Singular satisfiers tend to satisfy one specific need. They are neutral in relation to the satisfaction of other needs. Synergic satisfiers satisfy a given need, "simultaneously stimulating and contributing to the fulfillment of other needs" (Max-Neef et al., 1991, p. 34).

In the context of Max-Neef's model, we propose that Fixer behavior, like addictive behavior, can be understood as violators or destroyers and pseudo-satisfiers. Addictive behavior is always directed at satisfying a need, but what differentiates addictive behavior (violators or destroyers) from other methods (or other satisfiers) of meeting needs is that it paradoxically destroys the individual's capacity to meet the need(s) as well as their capacity to meet other needs. As an addictive lifestyle progresses, an individual's capacity to have most of his or her needs met is diminished, until there is a near-total reliance on the substance or addictive behavior (Fixer) to meet most fundamental human needs.

The above discussion highlights that developing a recovery program and lifestyle is a process of replacing destroyers/violators with synergistic and singular satisfiers as our methods for getting our fundamental needs met. In other words, from a Recovery Resilience Program perspective, we need to change having our needs met through our Fixer-driven behavior to meeting them through behaviors grounded in Natural Functioning. When we are in Naturally Functioning it is more likely that we can have our needs fulfilled through healthy means. Conversely, when we are in I-System Functioning, our Fixer-driven behavior (like substance use) will not meet our needs adequately, especially in the long run, no matter how hard we try. Rather, we will always be left feeling unfulfilled and dissatisfied.

Recovery Resilience Journal

Now that we have introduced the Depressor and Fixer you can include those I-System components into your daily journal. It is important to have an awareness of how your daily activities are influenced by the Depressor and Fixer.

Recovery Resilience Journal (Example)

	Addicted Mode Warning Signs	Requirements	Depressor/ Fixer Activity	Recovery Resilience Practice
Self	Feeling bummed out	I should not feel sad	Depressor: I will always feel sad What's the point of living sober Fixer: Daydreaming about times when I didn't feel sad while using	Defuse Depressor and Fixer Storylines Used Sensory Awareness to shift to Natural. Functioning
Others	Angry at my boss for not promoting me	My boss should reward my hard work	Depressor: My boss couldn't care less about me Fixer: Fantasizing about how I will tell him off	Defuse Depressor and Fixer Storylines Shifted to Natural Functioning & got on with my workday
The World	Ruminating about the political situation, politicians	Politicians should listen to and do what's best for their constituents	Depressor: Politicians are going to ruin the economy and cause me to lose my job Fixer: Spend time surfing and posting on social media	Defuse Depressor and Fixer Storylines Stopped wasting time on social media and helped a friend

Recovery Resilience Journal

	Addicted Mode Warning Signs	Requirements	Depressor/ Fixer Activity	Recovery Resilience Practice
Self				
Others				
The World				

SUMMARY OF CHAPTER 3

Recovery Resilience Practice

- Do **Mapping** related to any high-risk situation, trigger or troubling experience.
- **Recognize I-System Activity** by being aware of body tension and mental clutter.
- **Practice Sensory Awareness**.
- **Recognize Requirements** when performing daily activities.
- **Defuse Depressor Storylines**.
- **Defuse Fixer Storylines**.
- **Experience the Shift**.
- Complete your Recovery Resilience Journal daily.

On the next few pages please fill out the following:

Addicted Mode Warning Signs: Use the template and write down in the space provided your Addicted Mode Warning Signs for the past week. Try and be as comprehensive as possible.

Flourishing Scale: Complete the scale and calculate and your score, from 1 to 7, for each question over the past week or two.

Recovery Resilience Practice Scale: Complete the scale and calculate and write down the frequency of your Recovery Resilience Practice. Indicate whether it was never, hardly ever, occasionally, or regularly.

Addicted Mode Warning Signs

Date: _____

Over the past week write down how your I-System has been active in each of your life dimensions.

	Addicted Mode Warning Signs
Self	
Others	
The World	

Flourishing Scale

Date: _____

Below are eight statements with which you may agree or disagree. Using the 1–7 scale below, indicate your agreement with each item by indicating that response for each statement.

- 7 – Strongly agree
- 6 – Agree
- 5 – Slightly agree
- 4 – Neither agree nor disagree
- 3 – Slightly disagree
- 2 – Disagree
- 1 – Strongly disagree

Indicate your agreement with each item	(1–7)
I lead a purposeful and meaningful life	
My social relationships are supportive and rewarding	
I am engaged and interested in my daily activities	
I actively contribute to the happiness and well-being of others	
I am competent and capable in the activities that are important to me	
I am a good person and live a good life	
I am optimistic about my future	
People respect me	
Total score:	_____

The *Flourishing Scale* was developed by Diener, E., Wirtz, D., Tov, W., et al. (2010). New measures of well-being: Flourishing and positive and negative feelings. *Social Indicators Research*, 39, 247–266.

Recovery Resilience Practice Scale

Date: _____

Over the past week indicate the frequency of your Recovery Resilience Practice. Check the description that most closely reflects your practice: never, hardly ever, or occasionally.

Frequency of Recovery Resilience Practice	Never	Hardly Ever	Occasionally	Regularly
Recognize I-System Activity				
Mapping				
Sensory Awareness				
Recognize Requirements				
Defuse Depressor Storylines				
Defuse Fixer Storylines				
Experience the Shift				

4

• • • • • • • • •

Break the Addiction Cycle

Addiction, whatever its form, has always been a desperate search, on a false and hopeless path, for the fulfilment of human freedom.

Medard Boss, *Existential Foundations of Medicine and Psychology*

The Recovery Resilience Program outlined in this workbook can be understood as a strengths-based approach because it highlights an individual's self-determination, focuses on their innate strengths, and promotes individuals in recovery seeing themselves as resourceful and resilient in the face of adverse conditions.[1]

Chapter 3 highlighted that to sustain resilience when confronted with cravings and temptations that often accompany a recovery process, understanding Depressor and Fixer activity is imperative. This is not only crucial to preventing relapse and to building recovery resilience but also in improving your quality of life. As you learn more healthy coping skills and develop a Recovery Resilience Practice, you will begin to rely less on unhealthy Fixer behaviors.

A key aspect of a Recovery Resilience Practice is understanding the **Depressor-Fixer Cycle**. The Depressor-Fixer Cycle refers to the way the Depressor and Fixer interact with each other. Whenever there is Depressor activity there will be Fixer activity and vice versa. In this chapter, you will see how the Depressor-Fixer Cycle operates in and interferes with your day-to-day living, as well as how it can lead to a lapse and/or relapse. Recognizing the Depressor-Fixer

Cycle helps you to lessen the power your I-System has over you and can assist you in breaking the cycle of addiction.

The Depressor-Fixer Cycle

The Depressor and Fixer "dance" with each other, keeping you in an addicted mode and/or creating additional, internal distress in your life. The dynamics of the Depressor-Fixer Cycle may help explain why many of your attempts to reach certain goals have either failed or did not seem good enough even when you reached them. Your Depressor responds to a violated Requirement by spinning storylines about how you, others, or the world are broken, damaged or not good enough. Your Fixer comes up with never-ending fantasy-driven storylines that focus on how to fix yourself, others, and the world. Your Fixer tends to bring a sense of urgency and pressure to your activities. Moreover, no matter what you accomplish, the Depressor is ever-present to remind you that it was not good enough. As long as your Depressor spins storylines about some type inadequacy, your Fixer is going to overcompensate for that perceived inadequacy. Figure 1 illustrates the Depressor-Fixer Cycle.

In Chapter 1 we discussed how individuals with ineffective coping responses will experience decreased self-efficacy. This self-perception, together with the expectation that the use of a substance will have a positive effect (i.e., positive outcome expectancies), may well lead directly to an initial lapse back into addictive behavior. This lapse, in turn, often results in feelings of shame and failure (i.e., abstinence violation effect). In Figure 2 we show how the Depressor-Fixer Cycle manifests when in an addicted mode and how it could lead to a lapse and then full-blown relapse – and as anybody who has struggled with addictive behavior knows, once one is trapped in the addicted mode cycle it is very difficult to break, and it takes on a life of its own.

In Exercise 4.1, you will have the opportunity to explore in detail a situation that activated your Depressor-Fixer Cycle. In the space provided write down a situation that really got your I-System going (i.e., where you experienced significant mental clutter and body tension). The situation may represent a high-risk situation, trigger, or any troubling situation.

In each of the boxes describe the progression of your Depressor-Fixer Cycle activity related to this situation. An example is provided.

Figure 1 Depressor-Fixer Cycle.

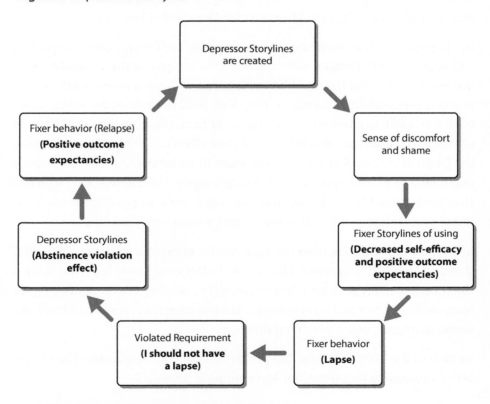

Figure 2 The addicted mode's Depressor-Fixer Cycle.

Example

Situation: I ran into someone I drank with in the past and started to crave alcohol.

Requirement: I should not have such strong cravings.

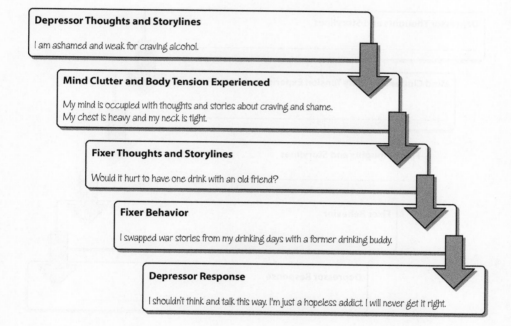

Depressor Thoughts and Storylines

I am ashamed and weak for craving alcohol.

Mind Clutter and Body Tension Experienced

My mind is occupied with thoughts and stories about craving and shame.
My chest is heavy and my neck is tight.

Fixer Thoughts and Storylines

Would it hurt to have one drink with an old friend?

Fixer Behavior

I swapped war stories from my drinking days with a former drinking buddy.

Depressor Response

I shouldn't think and talk this way. I'm just a hopeless addict. I will never get it right.

Situation: I ran into someone I drank with in the past and started to crave alcohol.

Requirement: I should not have such strong cravings.

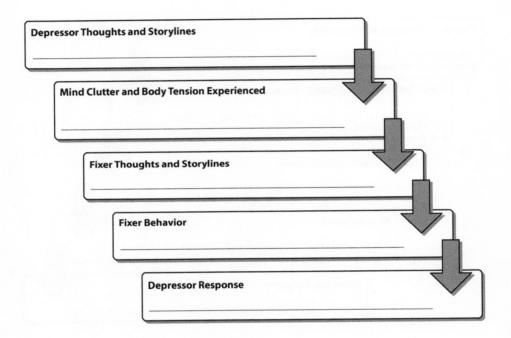

Depressor Thoughts and Storylines
_____

Mind Clutter and Body Tension Experienced
_____

Fixer Thoughts and Storylines
_____

Fixer Behavior
_____

Depressor Response
_____

When you contemplate your life do you recognize how pervasive your Depressor-Fixer Cycle has been over the years? Do you see how that cycle has played a role in maintaining your addiction as well as in some of your daily activities? In the next two exercises (4.2 and 4.3) you will write down how your Depressor-Cycle has interfered with your life in general and how it has played a role in sustaining your addiction.

I-System or Natural Functioning – Your Choice

Through a Recovery Resilience Practice, you have the capacity and choice to break your Depressor-Fixer Cycle and live your life guided by Natural Functioning. In Figure 3 we show the two possible paths or loops that can mediate your experiences: I-System Functioning and Natural Functioning. This diagram highlights that when your I-System is not active you automatically inhabit a Natural Functioning state. In this state, you are naturally resourceful, creative, psychologically flexible, and resilient, and in this state you can more readily access your recovery capital.

When a Requirement is violated, the I-System hijacks your Natural Functioning, filling your mind with storylines and your body full of tension, and distorting how you perceive, think, feel, and act. This is often the cause of your poor decisions and suffering, and many of your dysfunctional mind-body states, including your addicted mode.

As we have discussed, you have the capacity to alter which mind-body state you are in – Natural Functioning or I-System Functioning. The primary focus of a Recovery Resilience Practice is on recognizing when you are in the I-System mode and addicted mode and shifting to the Natural Functioning mode. Now obviously that is easier said than done. You will very often slip into the I-System loop without realizing it. The good news is that with practice you will become more aware of your I-System's signals (mental clutter and body tension) and increase your capacity to use your I-System as a compass that shifts you to get back on your Naturally Functioning course. In this Natural Functioning mode, you can more fully draw on your recovery capital to deal with high-risk situations as well as your day-to-day activities.

Write down in the space below how your Depressor-Fixer Cycle has interfered with your life. Try to write down specific examples.

_____

_____

_____

_____

_____

_____

_____

_____

_____

_____

_____

_____

_____

_____

_____

_____

_____

_____

_____

_____

_____

_____

_____

_____

_____

_____

_____

_____

_____

_____

_____

_____

_____

_____

_____

_____

_____

_____

_____

Write down in the space below how the Depressor-Fixer Cycle has contributed to your addictive behavior.

_____

_____

_____

_____

_____

_____

_____

_____

_____

_____

_____

_____

_____

_____

_____

_____

_____

_____

_____

_____

_____

_____

_____

_____

_____

_____

_____

_____

_____

_____

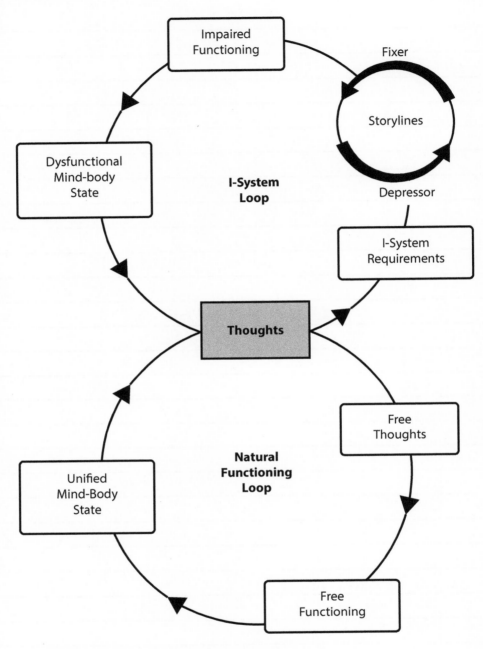

Figure 3 The I-System loop and the Natural Functioning loop.

The notion that we can change our mode of being is seen as a strengths-based approach, as it focuses on enhancing our abilities, knowledge, and capacities. Therefore, you don't have to be at the mercy of your I-System and addicted mode, as you have the strength and capacity to choose Natural Functioning in each activity of daily living.

A Change of Worldview

Addiction is characterized by cognitive distortions fueled by defense mechanisms like projection, denial, and/or repression (Brewer, 2017; West, 2017). Much of the therapeutic process of working a personal recovery program focuses on cognitive restructuring, which helps to work through defenses toward finding a more accurate perspective on the nature and consequences of addiction, as well as what life in recovery may look like. If you have completed a primary care process, then this was likely the main focus of this process.

A pivotal feature of moving from an addicted lifestyle to a recovery lifestyle is changing your worldview. Your worldview is how you understand yourself, others, and the world, and your place in society. As we have pointed out, the I-System, particularly its Depressor and Fixer Storylines, greatly influences or distorts your worldview. An addicted lifestyle is sustained by a worldview that rationalizes substance use. Alongside your other recovery practices, your Recovery Resilience Practice will change your worldview from one that sustained your addiction to one that sustains your recovery.

The exploration and transformation of one's worldview is a central feature within all Twelve-Step programs. In *It Works How and Why*, it states, "[W]e need to change how we perceive the world and alter our role in it" (Narcotics Anonymous World Services, 1983, p. 37). Carl Thune believes one of the reasons Alcoholics Anonymous and other Twelve-Step programs are effective is because its members share their life histories in Twelve-Step meetings and are "taught how to interpret their past in a way that gives meaning to the past and hope for the future" (in Flores, 1997,

p. 281). Thune states, highlighting the value of an alteration of worldview for an individual in recovery:

> In a sense, then, one of the first lessons AA must teach new members is that their lives were incoherent and senseless as they knew them. Simultaneously, it must reveal the "correct" understanding and interpretation of the drinking alcoholic's vision of the world before a new member can accept the full benefits of the program – a program which offers a different coherence and meaning to their active alcoholic lives. … More abstractly, it is not just a revised and now coherent vision of the world which AA offers, but one which has altered the relation between its components. (in Flores, 1997, p. 281)

Depressor and Fixer Storylines are supported by idealized and perfectionistic Requirements, which create a distorted view of ourselves, others, and the world. When you develop a worldview that is based in Natural Functioning, it strengthens your resilience and protects you from addicted mode thinking patterns – you perceive yourself, others and the world more realistically. Your life and your vision for the future become more meaningful – even the suffering of your past and your addiction become more meaningful within the fuller context of your life and recovery. Viktor Frankl (1953) believed that when we can place our suffering within some meaningful context or worldview, we are not defeated by it, but are helped to transcend it. Similarly, in AA members share "the kinship of suffering" and recovery depends on the mutual sharing of suffering. AA teaches the alcoholic that to be fully human is to need others and provides alcoholics with a universally shared explanation for their suffering. Flores (1997, p. 280) states that "[w]ith Socrates, we argue to 'know thyself.' In this fashion, AA members are taught to believe that the authentic existence advocated by the AA program holds the key to self-examination, self-knowledge, emancipation, cure, and eventual salvation."

Again and again, the authors have observed clients in recovery humbly acknowledging an existential shift in worldview and some version of the following: "Were it not for my prior addiction, and now committed recovery, I would not be nearly the person I am today. And for that, I am immensely grateful." Simply put, their past suffering has now become meaningful within a newfound worldview.

Finding Meaning in Life

When people have a personal meaning to their life, they are far less likely to engage in addictive behaviors (Du Plessis, 2019b). Viktor Frankl (1953) proposed that people are driven to search for a sense of meaning in their lives and that people without a sense of meaning in their lives experience an "existential vacuum," a state largely characterized by boredom and purposelessness. Substance use represents an inadequate and often self-destructive coping mechanism to escape the feelings associated with meaningless, inner pain, and boredom resulting from Frankl's existential vacuum, and addiction can be understood as a misguided quest for meaning. As Medard Boss (1983, p. 283) noted in the epigraph of this chapter, "Addiction, whatever its form, has always been a desperate search, on a false and hopeless path, for the fulfilment of human freedom."

The Italian Jungian practitioner Luigi Zoja echoes a similar sentiment, highlighting the existential motives that may drive substance use, "It is almost impossible for many young people to feel in any way useful in today's society. Why should we be so amazed that so many take drugs, and why should we interpret addiction as a regressive renunciation of the ego when the person making this choice is actually seeking a few moments of heroic identity?" (Zoja, 1989, pp. 15–16).

For recovery to be sustainable, one needs to develop a worldview that has a clear sense of meaning and purpose. With a Recovery Resilience Practice, your worldview will systemically shift to one that resonates with Natural Functioning. Right at the center of such a transformed worldview will be a personal foundation of meaning, values, and purpose that serves you well in a sustained, successful recovery. Viktor Frankl (1953, p. 84) in his book, *Man's Search for Meaning*, quotes Friedrich Nietzsche: "He who has a *why* to live [personal meaning and value and purpose] can bear with almost any *how*," which highlights how having a meaningful worldview is essential for developing the resilience needed for sustained recovery.

One of the unfortunate features of the Fixer is that it can influence what we find meaningful (your "whys") and taint it with perfectionistic and idealized outcomes. In the same way, your Fixer can taint your recovery goals. It is important to be mindful of this because instead of your life and recovery goals bringing you joy, they can become a source of anxiety and never-ending disappointment.

In Exercise 4.4 you are going to write down meaningful pursuits and goals and explore whether any have been tainted or even hijacked by your I-System. In the space provided, write down your goals. Then ask yourself what Requirements do I have about these goals? Remember that Requirements are mental rules your I-System creates regarding how you think you, others, or the world should be. Write these Requirements next to your goal. Then write the Depressor and Fixer Storylines that are associated with the Requirements in the third and fourth columns. Note the body tension you experience in connection with the Depressor Storylines.

It must be noted that it is entirely normal for your goals to be influenced by your I-System, but the aim here is to become aware of when the pursuit of goals becomes predominately Fixer-driven. You can know when a goal is Fixer-driven when you experience a disproportionate sense of urgency coupled with body tension and mental clutter associated with it. Conversely, when a goal is set and pursued in Natural Functioning, you are more likely to have realistic expectations and may also enjoy the process of striving toward the goal, and not simply be hyper-focused on its outcome.

Recovery Resilience Practice in Activities of Daily Living

Now let's look at some examples of how you can apply your Recovery Resilience Practice throughout the day. As we stress throughout this workbook, the arena of your practice is your activities of daily living and the activity of your I-System (i.e., its signals: body tension and mental clutter) can function like a compass that tells you when you are off course.

Goal	Requirements	Depressor Storylines	Fixer Storylines
Get fit	I must do it quickly	You will fail at it like most things	I will work out five times a week

Example

Situation: Argument with Jill.

Signal of My I-System Activity: Raised voice, chest pressure, tense body, jaw clenched, racing thoughts, and pressured speech.

Impact of I-System Activity: Not listening, argumentative, overexplaining.

Apply RRP: Defused Fixer Storyline: "make her understand." Recognized Requirement: *"she should understand."*

Benefits of RRP: Body relaxed, spoke with Jill without anger.

Example

Situation: Argument with Jack.

Signal: Wanting distance, sinking stomach, feeling hurt.

Impact of I-System Activity: Overly critical, verbally fighting back.

Apply RRP: Noticed my Depressor/Fixer Cycle. Recognized my Requirement: *"he should love me."* Defused Depressor Storyline: *"if he loved me, he wouldn't say hurtful things to me";* and Defused Fixer Storyline: *"I should teach him a lesson."*

Benefits of RRP: Still disappointed but less hurt, less devastated. More able to clearly express my opinion about the focus of the argument.

Recovery Resilience Journal

Now that we have introduced the Depressor-Fixer Cycle you can now include these I-System components/dynamics into your daily journal.

Example

Recovery Resilience Journal

	Addicted Mode Warning Signs	Requirements	Depressor/ Fixer Activity	Recovery Resilience Practice
Self	Thinking about skipping 12-Step meeting	I should always want to go to meetings	D: I must not be committed to my recovery. F: I'll find even more meetings to attend	Defuse Depressor and Fixer Storylines. Recognized Requirement. Returned focus to what I needed to do in that moment
Others	Argument with partner	My partner should agree with me	D: My partner does not support me, never takes my side. F: I just won't talk to her about this situation	Defuse Depressor and Fixer Storylines. Recognized Requirement. Was able to have a productive discussion with partner
The World	Ruminating about how life is unfair, meaningless after watching a documentary	Life should be fair and meaningful	D: Life is pointless. Good people get the short end of the stick. Bad people get all the breaks. F: Have a "screw it" attitude toward life. Be apathetic	Defuse Depressor and Fixer Storylines. Recognized Requirement. Able to see life as it is — there is good and bad, beauty and ugliness, suffering and joy

Recovery Resilience Journal

	Addicted Mode Warning Signs	Requirements	Depressor/ Fixer Activity	Recovery Resilience Practice
Self				
Others				
The World				

SUMMARY OF CHAPTER 4

Recovery Resilience Practice

- Do **Mapping** related to any high-risk situation, trigger, or troubling experience.
- **Recognize I-System Activity** by being aware of body tension and mental clutter.
- **Practice Sensory Awareness**.
- **Recognize Requirements** when performing daily activities.
- **Defuse Depressor Storylines.**
- **Defuse Fixer Storylines**.
- Recognize your **Depressor-Fixer Cycle** in activities of daily living.
- **Experience the Shift.**
- Complete your Recovery Resilience Journal daily.

On the next few pages please fill out the following:

Addicted Mode Warning Signs: Use the template and write down in the space provided your addicted mode warning signs for the past week. Try and be as comprehensive as possible.

Flourishing Scale: Complete the scale and calculate and your score, from 1 to 7, for each question over the past week or two.

Recovery Resilience Practice Scale: Complete the scale and calculate and write down the frequency of your Recovery Resilience Practice. Indicate whether it was never, hardly ever, occasionally, or regularly.

Addicted Mode Warning Signs

Date: _____

Over the past week write down how your I-System has been active in each of your life dimensions.

	Addicted Mode Warning Signs
Self	
Others	
The World	

Flourishing Scale

©Copyright by Ed Diener and Robert Biswas-Diener, January 2009

Date: _____

Below are eight statements with which you may agree or disagree. Using the 1–7 scale below, indicate your agreement with each item by indicating that response for each statement.

- 7 – Strongly agree
- 6 – Agree
- 5 – Slightly agree
- 4 – Neither agree nor disagree
- 3 – Slightly disagree
- 2 – Disagree
- 1 – Strongly disagree

Indicate your agreement with each item	(1–7)
I lead a purposeful and meaningful life	
My social relationships are supportive and rewarding	
I am engaged and interested in my daily activities	
I actively contribute to the happiness and well-being of others	
I am competent and capable in the activities that are important to me	
I am a good person and live a good life	
I am optimistic about my future	
People respect me	
Total score:	_____

The *Flourishing Scale* was developed by Diener, E., Wirtz, D., Tov, W., et al. (2010). New measures of well-being: Flourishing and positive and negative feelings. *Social Indicators Research*, 39, 247–266.

Recovery Resilience Practice Scale

Date: _____

Over the past week indicate the frequency of your Recovery Resilience Practice. Check the description that most closely reflects your practice: never, hardly ever, or occasionally.

Frequency of Recovery Resilience Practice	Never	Hardly Ever	Occasionally	Regularly
Recognize I-System Activity				
Mapping				
Sensory Awareness				
Recognize Requirements				
Defuse Depressor Storylines				
Defuse Fixer Storylines				
Experience the Shift				

5

. . . .

The Requirements That
Bind Us

Most substance-addicted people are also addicted to thinking, meaning they have a compulsive and unhealthy relationship with their own thinking.

David Foster Wallace, *Infinite Jest*

The "Big Book" of Alcoholics Anonymous states that "Resentment is the 'number one' offender. It destroys more alcoholics than anything else" (Wilson, 1976, p. 64). When we look at the etymology of the word "resentment" it derives from "re-sentiment," with "re" indicating something repeating itself and "sentiment" related to feeling. Resentment can thus be understood quite literally as "feeling again," especially in terms of the habitual recycling of perceived injustices toward us and their accompanying feelings. This mental habit of resentment has a significant cost psychologically and even physically, yet ironically does next to nothing to aid the resolution or closure of the original event. Simply put, resentment binds us in a kind of emotional enslavement to the offending person or event. It should come as no big surprise then that the root word in Latin, *addictus*, means "bond servant" or "slave." Hence, addiction might best be understood as being bound or enslaved by any substance, behavior, or attitude that is ultimately self-defeating in the long term.

According to Alcoholics Anonymous, what fuels resentment is having expect-ations. In Twelve-Step programs, members are warned about the danger that holding expectations has for their recovery. This sentiment is expressed by the slogan: "Expectations are premeditated resentments" (Wilson, 1976, p. 45). As pointed out in Chapter 1, we made a distinction between natural expectations and I-System Requirements. A key insight of the Recovery Resilience Program is that when you are faced with a situation that violates one or more of your Requirements, your I-System becomes active. Akin to the Twelve-Step philoso-phy, we argue that these Requirements will fuel your addicted mode and that recognizing them will take away much of their power to do so. The "Big Book" observes: "My serenity is inversely proportional to my expectations. The higher my expectations of other people are, the lower is my serenity. I can watch my serenity level rise when I discard my expectations" (Wilson, 1976, p. 45).

In addition to fueling resentments, Requirements also affect how we relate to potential high-risk situations, triggers, and stressful events in general. Chapter 1 of this workbook highlighted that oftentimes it is not the situation or event itself that creates your emotional distress, but the Requirements you have (often automatically and outside your awareness) for the situation. Thus, your Recovery Resilience Practice does not focus on changing any given situation (crucial insofar as many distressful situations or triggers may be unavoidable) but focuses instead on changing the "who" you bring to that situation – your Natural Functioning self or your I-System Functioning self.

You will find clear antecedents for this concept from the ancient Stoic philos-ophers, Marcus Aurelius, Seneca, and Epictetus. For example, in his *Meditations*, Marcus Aurelius writes, "If you are pained by any external thing, it is not this thing that disturbs you, but your own judgment about it. And it is in your power to wipe out this judgment now" (in Kaufman, 1997, p. 63). Similarly, in *It Works: How and Why: The Twelve Steps and Twelve Traditions of Narcotics Anonymous* – in a discussion of Step Four and taking ownership of our resentments – it states "[we] need to change how we perceive the world and alter our role in it" (Narcotics Anonymous World Services, 1983, p. 37). The good news is that through your Recovery Resilience Practice, you will "change how you perceive the world" by simply living your day-to-day life in Natural Functioning which brings with it the ability to cope in more optimal ways with triggers, high-risk and other distressing situations. As you experi-ence this shift from an I-System Functioning mode to a Natural Functioning mode many times throughout your day, you will gradually change your perception of yourself, others, and the world to one that is no longer dominated by self-defeating expectations.

Requirements and Suffering

The human experience includes various degrees of suffering, distress, and trauma (Badenoch, 2017; Maté, 2011; Winhall, 2021). These are unavoidable. However, a significant portion of this suffering – the part over which you have considerable control – is due to Requirements you have concerning how you, others, and the world should be.

The I-System can either cause suffering where none is warranted or add unnecessary suffering to an already distressing situation. When you practice the recognition of Requirements, your distress related to any situation will often be reduced to a sizable degree or may, in some circumstances, even melt away entirely as your I-System releases its hold on you. When you shift to a state of Natural Functioning, you will be in a more optimal position to deal with the situation, either in the form of an action or perhaps, instead, a nonaction, that is, accepting the situation as it is (often referred to as "letting go" in the recovery community).

The Twelve-Step Program, Buddhist and Stoic philosophy all share the perspective that suffering is caused by our unwillingness to accept the world as it is and our insistence on trying to make it fit our expected ideas or fantasies. Addiction is, in essence, a refusal to accept things as they are and an attempt to avoid the reality of necessary suffering (unavoidable existential experiences of loss, disappointment, boredom, struggle to find and maintain meaning in one's life, etc.). This refusal to accept things as they are leads to disproportionate need for control – a central feature of addictive dynamics. Ulman and Paul (2006) indicate how at the core of addiction dynamics, there is a fantasy of having an unrealistic sense of control of oneself, others, and things/events in the world:

> In the case of addiction, such a narcissistic fantasy centers on a narcissistic illusion of a megalomaniacal being that possesses magical control over psychoactive agents (things and activities). These latter entities

allow for the artificial alteration of the subjective reality of one's sense of one's self and one's personal world. Under the influence of these intoxicating fantasies, an addict imagines being like a sorcerer or wizard who controls a magic wand capable of manipulating the forces of nature – and particularly the forces of human nature. Eventually, a person becomes a captive of these addictive fantasies and then becomes an addict, lost in a wonderland. (p. 6)

In recovery we learn that there are various aspects of our being-in-the-world in which we are not in control, and this is not something to be ashamed about – but rather as something which makes us human. An important aspect of recovery is realizing the inevitability of suffering and letting go of our unrealistic demands. Flores (1997, pp. 195–196) highlights this shift for an individual in recovery:

> [m]any existential writers believe that in such a confrontation between the realistic acceptance of the world as it is and the self-centered demands for unlimited gratification [self-centered focus of I-System narratives], reason would prevail and the individual would choose more realistically between the [two distinct] alternatives: continued unhappy struggles with old patterns of expectations [Requirements] or authentic existence with expanded freedom of choice and responsible expression of drives and wishes [Natural Functioning].

Requirements and Motivation

In Chapters 1 and 2, we saw how Requirements underlie high-risk or triggering situations. When these Requirements are unmet or violated, they activate your I-System, making you more prone to entering into an addicted mode where cravings are amplified. Thus, you can begin to gain an appreciation for how helpful, even vital, it is to be able to Recognize Requirements in your activities of daily living.

Maintaining positive motivation is a crucial factor in sustained recovery and relapse prevention. Sadly, your Requirements often directly reduce your motivation for continued abstinence or working a truly successful personal recovery program.

It may be helpful here if we further unpack this concept of motivation as it relates to recovery. Motivation informs relapse prevention, by means of two antagonistic principles at war within the psyche of the addicted individual: (1) motivation for positive behavior change (choosing *not* to drink or use) versus (2) motivation to engage in the problematic behavior (choosing *to* drink or use).

The Requirements one has for one's recovery process can lead to disappointment or even shame. For example, individuals that have made a commitment to recovery may have the Requirement that once they have made this commitment, they should not experience cravings. Yet, when they experience triggers, high-risk situations, or stress, cravings may return. When this happens, the I-System will, if the Requirement is not recognized, become overactive – paving the way for their addicted mode to manifest. This means that Recognizing Requirements is essential for the "long haul" of lifelong recovery.

Defusing Requirements in the Moment

Recognizing Requirements while doing Mapping is very useful and makes you aware of Requirements that may arise in similar future situations. When Mapping, you may experience an "aha" when you recognize a Requirement. However, this is not the end but rather the beginning of this part of your practice. The Requirement will likely arise again when you encounter the same situation. The fact that you have recognized a Requirement via Mapping will help you recognize and defuse that Requirement when it surfaces again, allowing you to face that situation in Natural Functioning. To effectively deal with Requirements is to recognize them as they arise "in the heat of the moment." We call this **Defuse Requirements**. When you Defuse Requirements when they come up, you shift to Natural Functioning. Requirements are like the fuse in a stick of dynamite. If the fuse is lit (a Requirement is violated), but then is quickly cut before it can ignite the dynamite (Requirement is recognized and defused), the dynamite remains inert (the I-System continues to rest, and Natural Functioning prevails).

Although all Requirements are essentially the same in terms of the role they play in activating the I-System, it can be useful to categorize them. A simple way to classify the various types of Requirements is under the categories of: (1) Requirements for self; (2) Requirements for others; and (3) Requirements for the world. In Exercise 5.1, you will practice recognizing all three types of Requirements. As you complete these exercises, keep in mind that you can only defuse a Requirement "in the heat of the moment."

Requirements for Self

In Exercise 5.1, you are going to look at any high-risk situations or triggers related to your attitudes (e.g., self-pity, being ungrateful, resentment), thinking (euphoric recall, etc.), emotional states (anger, sadness, excitement, etc.), and behavior (overworking, withdrawing, etc.) that have in the past or could in the future activate your I-System and possibly lead to an addicted mode. In the chart in Exercise 5.1, list some of the most distressing high-risk situations or triggers that could activate your I-System. Then write down how you normally act in the high-risk situation or when encountering the situation or trigger. We provide an example to help you see how to complete the exercise.

High-risk situation/trigger	How do I act
Anger	Say mean or hurtful things

Choose one of the high-risk situations or triggers from the chart in Exercise 5.1 that is the most distressing (i.e., has the most body tension and mental clutter associated with it). Write it inside the oval on the Map in Exercise 5.2. Then take a couple of minutes to scatter your thoughts and feelings about that situation around the outside of the oval. Don't edit or second-guess, just write down whatever thoughts come to mind. At the bottom of the Map, provide a description of your body tension. We provide an example of a completed Map. A blank Map template follows the example.

In Exercise 5.3, see if you can recognize on the Map you just completed any Requirements ("shoulds" or "musts") you have for **yourself** in connection to the high-risk situation. List them in the box provided. We provide a few examples connected to the example Map.

Now that you have recognized some of the Requirements you have for yourself, you can defuse them in real time as they arise in your daily activities. Recognizing and Defusing Requirements "in the heat of the moment" will prevent them from causing your I-System to become overactive.

Requirements for Others

The presence of consistent social support makes a major difference between a sustained recovery process or risk of relapse. Positive social support is correlated with long-term abstinence rates across several addictive behaviors whereas negative social support, either in the form of interpersonal conflict or social pressure to use substances, is correlated with an increased risk for relapse (Barber & Crisp, 1995).

Scholars who support the "self-medication hypothesis" maintain that addicts often struggle to regulate their feelings and self-esteem which dates back to suboptimal responsiveness in key relationships formed early in life (Levin, 1995). As a result, they may find themselves particularly prone to external sources of gratification like substance use in later life (Kohut, 1977).

Example

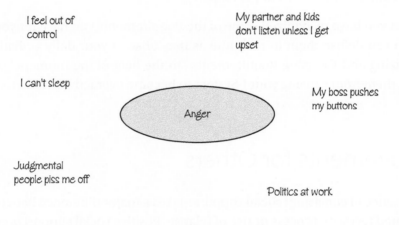

Situation Map (Example)

People are idiots

I feel out of
control

My partner and kids
don't listen unless I get
upset

I can't sleep

Anger

My boss pushes
my buttons

Judgmental
people piss me off

Politics at work

My partner
doesn't trust me

My "bad attitude" holds
me back at work

Description of body tension? <u>Chest gets tight. Clinched fists</u>

Situation Map

Description of body tension: _____

Requirements for self
I should not lose control
I should sleep better
I should have a better attitude

Khantzian (1999, p. 231) asserts that "[p]ersons with substance use disorders suffer in the extreme with their feelings, either being overwhelmed with painful affects or seeming not to feel their emotions at all. Substances of abuse help such individuals to relieve painful affects or to experience or control emotions when they are absent or confusing."

It is for this reason that the capacity to form healthy relationships is of utmost importance for an effective and sustainable recovery process. In fact, we often tell our clients that if many of their addictive patterns are rooted in failed attachments (including early caregiving relationships), then any genuine solution to said addiction must be currently grounded in healthy relational attachments.

According to Khantzian (1999), for addicts to develop a healthy and stable sense of self, they need to be in a supportive and empathically attuned social environment. He believes that only through this maintenance of solid connection with reliable others can the disorders of the self be repaired, which, from this relational (or attachment) point of view, lie at the root of addiction. That is why many believe that Twelve-Step programs provide the ideal environment for addicts to heal. For example:

> Ernst Kurtz views the mutuality of AA – one alcoholic needing and helping another – as the cornerstone of the recovery process and the main reason why twelve-step programs are so successful. Isolation of one's self from the rest of humanity is one consequence of shame and the driving force behind addiction, since the use of chemicals enhances the denial, fuels the grandiose defenses, and keeps one isolated. (in Flores, 1997, p. 245)

The various Twelve-Step fellowships provide easily accessible and well-established recovering communities. A Twelve-Step program infrastructure and community provide a space and culture where "[g]radually, alcoholics or addicts are able to give up the grandiose defenses (narcissism) and false-self persona for a discovery of self (true self) as they really are" (Flores, 1997, p. 293).

According to William White (1996, p. xxvii) participation in Twelve-Step fellowships helps the transition from the culture of addiction into the culture of recovery, an essential element for sustainable recovery. In addressing the need for a cultural transition as part of a recovery process he states that:

> Addiction and recovery are more than something that happens inside someone. Each involves deep human needs in interaction with a social environment. For addicts, addiction provides a valued cocoon where these needs can be, and historically have been, met [even if self-destructively]. No treatment can be successful if it doesn't offer an [alternate] pathway to meet those same needs and provide an alternative social world that has perceived value and meaning.

From the above discussion, it is clear that the quality of our relationships is imperative for sustained recovery. The Requirements we have for others can greatly influence the quality of our relationships. One of the biggest hindrances to forming healthy relationships is our Requirements for others. These "shoulds" or "musts" we hold for others often lead to disappointment and resentment and may eventually erode even our most valued relationships. Consequently, to maintain healthy relationships, which are imperative for sustained and successful recovery, we need to become aware of the Requirements we have for others, as they unfold in real time. Otherwise, our relationships, which are meant to be supportive, can become a significant trigger or high-risk situation for relapse.

In Exercise 5.4, we are going to look at situations or triggers related to your relationships (romantic partner, family, or friends) that have the potential to activate your I-System and possibly lead to an addicted mode.

In the chart below, list some of the situations or triggers related to your relationships that could activate your I-System. Then write down how you typically act when encountering the situation or trigger. We provide an example to help you see what to do.

Choose one of the high-risk situations or triggers from the above chart that is the most distressing (i.e., has the most body tension and mental clutter associated with it). Write it inside the oval on the Map in Exercise 5.5. Then take a

Situation/trigger	How do I act
Arguing with partner	Isolate

couple of minutes to scatter your thoughts and feelings about that situation around the outside of the oval. Don't edit or second-guess, just write down whatever thoughts come to mind. Provide a description of your body tension in the space provided at the bottom of the page. On the next page we provide an example of a completed Map for Exercise 5.5. A blank Map template follows the example.

In Exercise 5.6, see if you can recognize on the Map you just completed any Requirements ("shoulds" or "musts") you have for **others** in connection to the high-risk situation. List them in the box provided. We provide a few examples connected to the example Map.

Example

Situation Map (Example)

My partner
doesn't listen

My partner
always brings
up my past

We don't communicate

We never resolve
anything

Arguing with
my partner

My partner
gives me the

We say hurtful
things

My partner doesn't
care about me

My partner
pushes my
buttons

My partner doesn't try to
see it from my perspective

Description of body tension? <u>My stomach hurts and my face feels hot</u>

Situation Map

Description of body tension: _____

Requirements for others
My partner should not push my buttons
My partner should not give me the silent treatment
My partner should not bring up the past

Now that you have recognized some of the Requirements you have for others, you can defuse them in real time as they arise in your daily activities.

Defusing Requirements for the World

In Exercise 5.7, we are going to look at situations or triggers related to your environment (for example, your financial situation, political events, social and cultural events, world events) that have the potential to activate your I-System, possibly leading to an addicted mode.

In the chart below, list some of the situations and/or triggers related to your environment that could activate your I-System. Then write down how you typically act when encountering the situation or trigger.

Situation/trigger	How do I act
Need more money	Isolate

Choose one of the high-risk situations or triggers from the above chart that is the most distressing (i.e., has the most body tension and mental clutter associated with it). Write it inside the oval on the Map template for Exercise 5.8. Then take a couple of minutes to scatter your thoughts and feelings about that situation around the outside of the oval. Don't edit or second-guess, just write down whatever thoughts come to mind. Provide a description of your body tension in the space provided at the bottom of the page. On the next page, we provide an example of a completed Map for Exercise 5.8. A blank Map template follows the example.

In Exercise 5.9, see if you can recognize on the Map you just completed any Requirements ("shoulds" or "musts") you have for **the world** in connection to the high-risk situation. List them in the box provided. We provide a few examples connected to the example Map.

Example

Situation Map (Example)

Co-workers should
not play politics

The boss should
not play favorites

Promotions should go to
those who are most
qualified

People are fake

Problems at work

Frustrated with
company I work for

Quit and tell
them all how I
feel

Policies are unfair

I can't deal
with the politics

Request a transfer

Description of body tension? <u>Tight chest. Clinched teeth</u>

Situation Map

Description of body tension: _____

Requirements for the world
Policies should be fair
I should not be frustrated about things I can't control
Promotions should go to those who deserve them

Now that you have recognized some of the Requirements you have for "the world," you can defuse them in real time as they arise in your daily activities.

Practice Map

Now that we have introduced all the components of a Recovery Resilience Practice, you will have the opportunity to incorporate them all in doing a Map of a distressing situation. We want to emphasize that the primary focus of your Recovery Resilience Practice is your activities of daily living (i.e., recognizing I-System interference in your day-to-day life, moment by moment) but Mapping regularly is also very helpful because it helps you "see" your I-System in action.

We will outline a Mapping process which combines all the components of a Recovery Resilience Practice, and represents a comprehensive way of doing a Map.

Your Recovery Resilience Practice is:

1. Mapping
2. Recognize I-System Activity
3. Sensory Awareness
4. Recognize and Defuse Requirements
5. Defuse Depressor Storylines
6. Defuse Fixer Storylines
7. Experience the Shift

Each component of your Recovery Resilience Practice is indicated in **bold text**. An example Map is provided. Follow the instructions to complete your own Map using the templates provided.

For Exercise 5.10 choose a distressing situation that you are currently facing and write it inside the oval on the Map (**Mapping**). Take a couple of minutes to scatter your thoughts and feelings about that situation around the outside of the oval. Don't edit or second-guess, just write down whatever thoughts come to mind. When you've finished writing down your thoughts, write a description of your body tension in the allocated space below the Map (i.e., How much body tension am I experiencing? Where in my body do I notice any tension? How do I describe it?) (**Recognize I-System Activity**).

Identify (using the letter R) the Requirements you have about the situation (**Recognize Requirements**). (Remember that you can only defuse a Requirement when it pops up in the moment. Mapping helps you to be able to recognize a Requirement so that you can defuse it in real time.)

Identify (using the letter D) negative thoughts on your Map that have accompanied Depressor Storylines, and identify (using the letter F) any thoughts on your Map that have accompanied Fixer Storylines.

In Exercise 5.11 list the Requirements you identified on your Map in the space provided and also write down the Depressor and Fixer Storylines associated with the thoughts on your Map. We provide an example.

Now that you have written down your Depressor Storylines you can defuse them by labelling it. This can be done by saying: "I'm having a thought that _____." (**Defuse Depressor Storylines**)

In the same way you can defuse your Fixer Storylines by labelling it. This can be done by saying: "I'm having a thought that _____." (**Defuse Fixer Storylines**)

Becoming aware that your I-System is overactive due to a violated Requirement, and Defusing Depressor and Fixer Storyline allows you to befriend it, to use it as a compass that guides a shift to Natural Functioning. Focusing on your senses (**Sensory Awareness**) will also help facilitate this shift.

As you completed the Map and became more intimate with the dynamics of your I-System you likely experienced the **Shift** as you start inhabiting a Natural Functioning mode of being. You are now able to contemplate the situation or deal with it in a mode which allows for more flexibility, resilience, creativity, and a broader range of responses. You will recognize that the situation you are dealing with is the same – but the "**who**" that is dealing with it has shifted.

Recovery Resilience Journal

Now that we have introduced all the components of your Recovery Resilience Practice, you can now incorporate them in your Recovery Resilience journal.

Example

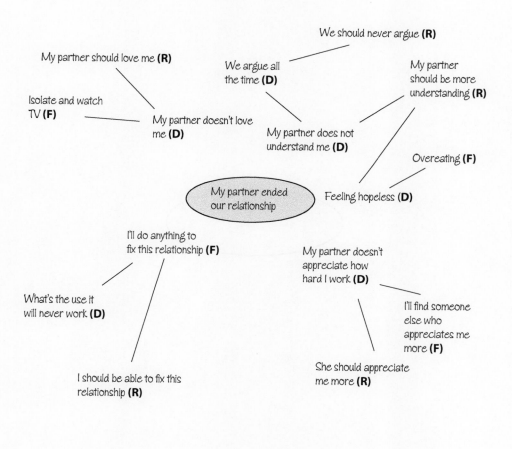

Mind-Body Map (Troubling Situation)

We should never argue **(R)**

My partner should love me **(R)**

We argue all the time **(D)**

My partner should be more understanding **(R)**

Isolate and watch TV **(F)**

My partner doesn't love me **(D)**

My partner does not understand me **(D)**

Overeating **(F)**

My partner ended our relationship

Feeling hopeless **(D)**

I'll do anything to fix this relationship **(F)**

My partner doesn't appreciate how hard I work **(D)**

What's the use it will never work **(D)**

I'll find someone else who appreciates me more **(F)**

I should be able to fix this relationship **(R)**

She should appreciate me more **(R)**

Description of body tension: <u>My chest is tight and heavy</u>

Mind-Body Map (Troubling Situation)

Description of body tension: _____

Requirement	Depressor Storyline(s)	Fixer Storyline(s)
My partner should appreciate me	My partner doesn't appreciate how hard I work	I'll find someone else who appreciates me

Example

Recovery Resilience Journal

	Addicted Mode Warning Signs	Requirements	Depressor/Fixer Activity	Recovery Resilience Practice
Self	Thinking about and regretting bad decisions made in the past.	I should not make bad decisions.	Replaying storylines about bad decisions made and how you might fix the damage they caused.	Sensory Awareness. Became aware of storylines. Recognized and Defused my Requirement. Felt the Shift. Returned my focus to the tasks at hand.
Others	Was angry at my coworker most of the day for sucking-up to the boss.	My coworker should not play politics.	Was distracted most of the day with thoughts about coworker (how he is wrong and how I can change his behavior), was not productive.	Recognized and Defused my Requirement. Sensory Awareness. Shifted to Natural Functioning. Able to focus on work.
The World	Argued with my boss about an unfair company policy, stewed about it all day.	Policies should be fair.	Spent time arguing instead of doing what needed to be done (Fixer). Spent time stewing about unfair policy. (Depressor)	Defused Depressor and Fixer Storylines. Mapped the situation. Recognized the Requirement that triggered my I-System.

Recovery Resilience Journal

	Addicted Mode Warning Signs	Requirements	Depressor/Fixer Activity	Recovery Resilience Practice
Self				
Others				
The World				

SUMMARY OF CHAPTER 5

Recovery Resilience Practice

- Do **Mapping** related to any high-risk situation, trigger, or troubling experience.
- **Recognize I-System Activity** by being aware of body tension and mental clutter.
- **Practice Sensory Awareness**.
- **Recognize & Defuse Requirements** when performing daily activities.
- **Defuse Depressor Storylines.**
- **Defuse Fixer Storylines**.
- Recognize your **Depressor-Fixer Cycle** in activities of daily living.
- **Experience the Shift.**
- Complete your Recovery Resilience Journal daily.

On the next few pages please fill out the following:

Addicted Mode Warning Signs: Use the template and write down in the space provided your Addicted Mode Warning Signs for the past week. Try and be as comprehensive as possible.

Flourishing Scale: Complete the scale and calculate and your score, from 1 to 7, for each question over the past week or two.

Recovery Resilience Practice Scale: Complete the scale and calculate and write down the frequency of your Recovery Resilience Skills practice. Indicate whether it was never, hardly ever, occasionally, or regularly.

Addicted Mode Warning Signs

Date: _____

Over the past week write down how your I-System has been active in each of your life dimensions.

	Addicted Mode Warning Signs
Self	
Others	
The World	

Flourishing Scale

Date: _____

Below are eight statements with which you may agree or disagree. Using the 1–7 scale below, indicate your agreement with each item by indicating that response for each statement.

- 7 – Strongly agree
- 6 – Agree
- 5 – Slightly agree
- 4 – Neither agree nor disagree
- 3 – Slightly disagree
- 2 – Disagree
- 1 – Strongly disagree

Indicate your agreement with each item	(1–7)
I lead a purposeful and meaningful life	
My social relationships are supportive and rewarding	
I am engaged and interested in my daily activities	
I actively contribute to the happiness and well-being of others	
I am competent and capable in the activities that are important to me	
I am a good person and live a good life	
I am optimistic about my future	
People respect me	
Total score:	_____

The *Flourishing Scale* was developed by Diener, E., Wirtz, D., Tov, W., et al. (2010). New measures of well-being: Flourishing and positive and negative feelings. *Social Indicators Research*, 39, 247–266.

Recovery Resilience Practice Scale

Date: _____

Over the past week indicate the frequency of your Recovery Resilience Practice. Check the description that most closely reflects your practice: never, hardly ever, or occasionally.

Frequency of Recovery Resilience Practice	Never	Hardly Ever	Occasionally	Regularly
Recognize I-System Activity				
Mapping				
Sensory Awareness				
Recognize Requirements				
Defuse Depressor Storylines				
Defuse Fixer Storylines				
Defuse Requirements				
Experience the Shift				

6

. . . .

Your Recovery Resilience Practice

Freedom is the most ineradicable craving of human nature.
Jan Smuts, *Holism and Evolution*

In Chapter Five we provided an overview of all aspects of a **Recovery Resilience Practice** that will contribute toward a sustainable recovery lifestyle. In this chapter you will consolidate your Recovery Resilience Practice and see how to use it to support any recovery program and pathway you choose. As highlighted throughout the workbook, the central aim of your Recovery Resilience Practice is to remove the hindrance that obstructs your capacity to access your recovery capital and apply recovery skills as well as provide a practice that can help you moment by moment to deal with stress, high-risk situation, triggers, or any troubling situations. In short, your Recovery Resilience Practice removes the hindrance to your innate resilience and capacity for flourishing and assists you in achieving your recovery and life goals. With a continued practice, your self-efficacy will grow, and this is important because higher levels of self-efficacy are predictive of improved substance use disorder treatment outcomes (Greenfield et al., 2000).

One of the central aims of any adequate addiction recovery process is to not only gain freedom from addiction but also to live up to our potential, to flourish. As we have highlighted in this workbook, having this freedom also requires us to understand and manage our I-Systems, which when overactive can lead to a relapse as well as to a limited state of being and an impaired way of relating to ourselves, others, and the world (i.e., addicted mode).

Freedom and Powerlessness

The concepts of "freedom" and "powerlessness" are frequently used in addiction treatment and recovery communities. South African philosopher and statesman Jan Smuts (1926, p. 321) asserted "[to] be a free personality represents the highest achievement of which any human being is capable." Addiction can be understood as a lifestyle that severely constricts our capacity for freedom, whereas a recovery lifestyle allows for a fuller expression of freedom and self-actualization. Recall how we earlier examined the etymology of the word "addiction," discovering it to be *addictus* (from the original Latin). *Addictus*, in the ancient Roman world, connoted being a bond servant, that is, someone bound in servitude to a master. If we explore the analogy to addictions, we can readily see how freedom is lost, as with a bond servant, in active addiction. And whatever recovery implies, it surely has as its primary foundation a return to freedom and choice.

Even though a person might have an addiction problem that limits their willpower in relation to the use of substances, known as "powerlessness" in Twelve-Step programs, it does not make them "powerless" over the choices they can make to get the right support and to follow practices that will prevent them from regressing into this "powerless" condition. Admitting one's powerlessness over the use of substances does not negate one's willpower to make choices that support either a recovery lifestyle or an addictive lifestyle. Philip Flores (1997, p. 273) highlights the positive existential implication for an individual in recovery accepting their powerlessness over substances and states that "[p]owerlessness over alcohol and the acceptance of one's limitation in relation to alcohol serves as a prototype for the alcoholic facing and accepting other limitations of the human condition."

Addiction can be understood as an attempt to bypass certain of our inherent limitations and fundamental human needs (recall our discussion of Max-Neef and how substance use can be a destructive means of having fundamental needs met). While in active addiction, individuals try to control the uncontrollable to avoid and self-medicate the natural human experiences of pain, disappointment, loss, and boredom. There are certain aspects of life that are within our capacity to control and manipulate, but there are also aspects that are simply given and cannot be avoided or controlled. Existential philosophers sometimes refer those things in life that we cannot change as "existential givens" (Yalom, 1995). At the core of addiction dynamics, there is a fantasy of having an unrealistic sense of control of oneself, others, and these "existential givens" where an individual "eventually becomes a captive of these addictive fantasies and then becomes an addict, lost in a wonderland" (Ulman & Paul, 2006, p. 6).

Through a recovery practice we not only aim to find freedom from our addiction, but also to find freedom and meaning within the limitations of our human condition. In a lifestyle that resonates with Natural Functioning, we step out of this "wonderland" and we gain more freedom while not trying to control the uncontrollable or striving to meet impossible to attain and perfectionistic demands that are imposed on us by our I-System. We simply see things more realistically and deal with life as it is, not with how we think it ought to be.

Recovery Resilience Analysis

The Recovery Resilience Program is based on the premise (like Twelve-Step philosophy) that addiction is a dysfunctional way of being and stopping the use of drugs is only one aspect of a sustainable recovery process. In short, one needs a complete lifestyle change – a change from a lifestyle dominated by an addicted mode to a lifestyle that resonates with Natural Functioning. Without a shift in lifestyle and access to recovery capital, the individual may eventually gravitate back to his or her habitual mode of being-in-the-world, that is, substance use. The Recovery Resilience Program, like Twelve-Step programs, views recovery as a "way of life" and "not a plan for recovery that can be finished and done with" and an approach to "living that allows for limitless expansion" (Wilson, 1976, p. 311).

We have seen that any activity is carried out in either the I-System or Natural Functioning mode. What is of primary importance is not only *what* you are doing, but *who* is doing it. That is, are your daily activities and goals driven by your I-System in an attempt to "fix" yourself or are they inspired by Natural Functioning? When your activities and goals are driven by your I-System, you will view yourself against the backdrop of unattainable and perfectionistic Requirements. Instead of improving your well-being, this adds to your distress and feelings of inadequacy and shame. Your Fixer will drive you relentlessly to fix these unpleasant and painful thoughts, feelings, and body sensations caused by the Depressor. And when your goals are achieved your Depressor will let you know that whatever you did was not good enough.

The Recovery Resilience Program is based on the premise that the more your daily activities are done in Natural Functioning the greater your recovery resilience will be – and that activities that are Fixer-driven make you more prone to lapse and relapse. However, it is not always obvious or easy to know when your activities are I-System driven and is acting as a hindrance to your innate resilience.

To assist you in gaining awareness of how your I-System can hinder your recovery lifestyle and keep you from achieving your goals, Exercise 6.1 will engage you in what we call a **Recovery Resilience Analysis.** A Recovery Resilience Analysis is a systematic and comprehensive exploration of how your I-System acts as a hindrance in your daily life. It involves exploring your relationship with yourself, others, and the world (environment), as well as how plans and goals may be influenced by your I-System. In short, the focus here is on how I-System activity manifests in your daily life and how it influences your activities and goals. The attention here is on the hindrance, not only on the practices, as our approach is based on the notion that your resilience naturally flourishes when the hindrance is removed. So, in one way your recovery resilience depends not only on what you do, but also to the extent to which the I-System is not interfering with what you do. That is to say, your recovery resilience is proportionately tied to your Recovery Resilience Practice (those moment by moment practices that quiet your I-System).

Performing a Recovery Resilience Analysis can help you see how your I-System is influencing your daily activities, relationships, and worldview.

Through the insight gained you can alter your worldview, improve your relationships, and adjust plans and goals so that they are more congruent with the life you actually desire and want to live, rather than a life driven by the I-System where nothing is ever good enough and you feel perpetually unfulfilled. When your life is I-System driven you are like a "hungry ghost" (using a phrase from addiction expert Gabor Maté, 2011) where, like a ghost, it does not matter how much you "eat," it falls right through you and never satisfies your hunger. In Natural Functioning you are more likely to use appropriate methods to meet your needs and feel satisfied.

A Recovery Resilience Analysis is akin to Step Four of the Twelve-Step program where one conducts a "moral inventory." In a Recovery Resilience Analysis, instead of focusing on the moral component and highlighting character defects, the focus is on I-System activity. A Recovery Resilience Analysis is in no way meant to replace a Step Four process as the focus of that process is different. However, making "a searching and fearless" inventory of I-System activity can be a good adjunct to a Step Four process for those in Twelve-Step programs.

To perform a **Recovery Resilience Analysis,** follow these instructions:

1. Using the templates provided on the next few pages complete a Map for each of these life domains: (1) self, (2) others, and (3) the world and your environment. Write any thoughts related to each domain that come to mind. Feel free to include thoughts about your various recovery practices (e.g., *I am lazy when it comes to Step Work, I am bored in meetings*). Write whatever comes to mind without editing.
2. Once you have completed the Maps, list the I-System activity related to the Map, write down your Requirements and Depressor and Fixer Storylines in the space provided.

Completing a Recovery Resilience Analysis will provide you with an insight of how I-System activity is interfering in the various domains of your life and with your recovery practices. Consequently, we recommend that you do this routinely as part of your Recovery Resilience Practice. And keep in mind that completing a Recovery Resilience Analysis will do you very little good unless you apply what you learn about your I-System in your daily life and continue to apply your Recovery Resilience Practice.

Example Map

Recovery Resilience Analysis Map for Self

I should never feel down

I should not need to smoke weed

I'm broken

I'll never accept myself as I am

Smoke Weed to find temporary relief

Isolate and watch TV

Self

I've never been able to focus on the positive, and never will

I am grumpy

I am going to start memorizing affirmations right now

I should be able to simply count my blessings, rather than complain all the time

Force myself to smile at people even though I often don't feel like it

I should be nicer to everybody

Map

Recovery Resilience Analysis Map for Self

Self

I-System activity for self

Requirements	
Depressor Storylines	
Fixer Storylines	

Example Map

Recovery Resilience Analysis Map for Others

My partner should love me

My partner shouldn't argue with me

My partner should be more understanding

We argue all the time

Isolate and watch TV

My partner does not understand me

Overeating

My partner doesn't love me

Others

People are mean

I'll tell my boss off

I'll find someone else who appreciates me more

I'll just quit my job

My boss doesn't appreciate how hard I work

People are two-faced

People shouldn't judge me

Recovery Resilience Analysis Map for Others

Others

I-System activity for others

Requirements	
Depressor Storylines	
Fixer Storylines	

Recovery Resilience Analysis Map for the World

The world is broken

Life should be fair

Trust nobody

My 12-step
program isn't
run right

I'll look for another
program

World

My community
should do more to
support recovery

This town is
boring

I need to move

My car shouldn't
break down

My employer should care
more about its employees

Recovery Resilience Analysis Map for the World

I-System activity for the world

Requirements	
Depressor Storylines	
Fixer Storylines	

Recovery Resilience Analysis Synopsis

In Exercise 6.7 you are going to complete a **Recovery Resilience Analysis Synopsis**. This provides a summary and integration of your Recovery Resilience Analysis.

List the Requirements and the Depressor and Fixer Storylines from your Recovery Resilience Analysis that pose the biggest risk to your recovery lifestyle.

You may notice that there is some commonality between the Requirements, Depressor and Fixer Storylines you have for self, others, and the world/environment.

Notice and write down any patterns you may find and consider how you can apply your Recovery Resilience Practice in your activities of daily living when you next encounter these same situations.

Once you have completed the Recovery Resilience Analysis and Synopsis, you will be more aware of how your I-System manifests in your life as well as how it may potentially hijack your various recovery practices. A Recovery Resilience Analysis can help you identify the aspects of your life that can benefit from using your Recovery Resilience Practice to remove what hinders (I-System overactivity) your innate resilience (e.g., *Defusing Requirements you have for your partner, Defuse Depressor Storylines about your job,* or *Defuse Fixer Storylines about your finances*).

As we have pointed out, any practice, even your recovery practices, can be hijacked by your I-System. So even if the healthiest of activities is I-System driven, it can have the opposite affect that it is designed to achieve or simply cause you to feel disappointment and shame.

For example, a central feature of Twelve-Step programs is the application of spiritual principles in our daily lives. This can be seen to be a similar approach to virtue ethics.[1] Virtue ethics is a philosophy developed by the Ancient Greek philosopher Aristotle. It is the quest to live a life of moral character. This character-based approach to morality assumes that we acquire virtue through practice (Peterson & Seligman, 2004). By practicing being honest, brave, just, generous, and so on, a person develops an honorable and

Recovery Resilience Analysis Synopsis

	Requirements	Depressor	Fixer
Self	I should never feel down	I'll never accept myself as I am	Smoke weed to find temporary relief
Others	My partner shouldn't argue with me	My partner will never accept me as I am	Isolate and watch TV
World	Life should be fair	The world is broken	Trust nobody

moral character. According to Aristotle, by honing virtuous habits, people will likely make the right choice when faced with ethical challenges. So, virtue ethics helps us understand what it means to be a virtuous human being. And it gives us a guide for living life without giving us specific rules for resolving ethical dilemmas.

Now the problem is that if our practice of virtues or spiritual principles is I-System driven, we will be held hostage by Requirements, and no matter how hard we try the Depressor will be there to tell us that we are not good enough. Failing to live up to these perfectionistic ideals will result in shame. Moreover, we could hold others accountable to unrealistic and perfectionistic virtuous or spiritual ideals, which can only lead to resentment and disappointment. A Recovery Resilience Analysis can thus help us to see from a more objective distance the degree to which our I-Systems are interfering with our ethical life and recovery practices and life goals.

In the same way that those who practice a Twelve-Step program incorporate a shortened version of Step Four as part of their Step Ten practice when completing a daily journal, a shortened version of a Recovery Resilience Analysis can be incorporated as part of your daily journal practice. The value of doing a daily journal as part of a recovery process is well-documented. Reflecting on the "who" (I-System or Natural Functioning) as well as the "what" (your daily activities) can greatly add to the benefit of this foundational recovery practice. As you become more aware of how your I-System interferes in your activities of daily living, you become better able to recognize it as it happens and simply being aware of your I-System's activities is often enough to get you back on track.

Step Eleven

The practice of meditation is central in Step Eleven of the Twelve-Step program where the suggestion is made to use "meditation to improve our conscious contact" (Wilson, 1976, p. 45) with a power greater than oneself. The focus of the suggestions made in Step Eleven is on gaining acceptance of things as they are and the capacity to deal with reality as it is. Step Eleven has congruence with the Stoic-influenced notion of *"amor fati"* as advocated by Friedrich Nietzsche. He states:

> I want to learn more and more to see as beautiful what is necessary in things; then I shall be one of those who makes things beautiful. *Amor fati:* let that be my love henceforth! I do not want to wage war against what is ugly. I do not want to accuse; I do not even want to accuse those who accuse. Looking away shall be my only negation. And all in all and on the whole: someday I wish to be only a Yes-sayer. (Nietzsche, 2003, p. 157)

Nietzsche clearly takes poetic license in his description of *"amor fati,"* and it may be an unattainable goal, but we can learn from his suggestion, as a pure practice of virtuous or spiritual principles is ultimately unattainable. That is, we never attain an attitude of unconditional acceptance but instead strive toward it. We can never be free from expectations and Requirements but instead strive toward minimizing their potentially destructive effects. It is our I-System's Fixer that demands perfection. In short, the aim of a practice like Step Eleven is to assist us in becoming more accepting of things that are beyond our control and not to try and "fix what isn't broke." French philosopher Simone de Beauvoir (1948) shares a similar notion in her expression of "ambiguity," which is that we are free but at the same time powerless over many things; that we are not totally free nor are we totally at the mercy of things. Our nature is ambiguous – as a central feature of our existence – and this ambiguity or tension is not to be regarded as a flaw that should be eliminated. Instead, she suggests that if "we do not succeed in fleeing it, let us, therefore, try to look the truth in the face. Let us try to assume our fundamental ambiguity. It is in the knowledge of the genuine conditions of our life that we must draw our strength of life and our reason for acting" (de Beauvoir 1948, p. 22).

Step Eleven is more closely related to Western traditions and techniques of philosophical contemplation than typical Eastern meditation practices, in that we seek to "improve our conscious contact." The aim is not detached awareness as is the case in most meditation practices, but insight. This aligns with a Recovery Resilience Practice where we become familiar with the workings of our minds.[2] The aim is to gain familiarity with, and to recognize, your I-System Storylines. Recall, that the premise of this workbook is that in a state of Natural Functioning, we unleash our innate resilience, inner wisdom, and resourcefulness. Thus, the goal here is not to gain decentered awareness of thoughts but rather to gain what the Greek philosophers called *phronesis* or practical wisdom. In short, the aim is to access your inner wisdom, which is found in Natural Functioning, which guides you on how to act and meet the imperative of the moment. Phronesis is concerned with particulars because it is concerned with how to act in particular situations. In a Natural Functioning state, we connect to a source of wisdom that is greater and deeper than our usual thinking patterns (and depending on your belief it may be that your source of inner wisdom is your True or Inner Self, Higher Power, or God). This is congruent with Step Eleven where the aim is to "improve our conscious contact." So, we suggest your Step Eleven practice can include an awareness and befriending of your I-System activity.

The philosopher Bertrand Russell provides a description of philosophical contemplation that resonates with our view of a Natural Functioning orientation toward existence – where we are not caught up in the self-centered vicissitudes of the I-System:

> The mind which has become accustomed to the freedom and impartiality of philosophic contemplation will preserve something of the same freedom and impartiality in the world of action and emotion. It will view its purposes and desires as parts of the whole, with the absence of insistence that results from seeing them as infinitesimal fragments in a world of which all the rest is unaffected by any one man's deeds. The impartiality which, in contemplation, is the unalloyed desire for truth, is the very same quality of mind which, in action, is justice, and in emotion is that universal love which can be given to all, and not only to those who are judged useful or admirable. Thus, contemplation enlarges not only the objects of our thoughts, but also the objects of our actions and our affections: it makes us citizens of the universe, not only of one walled city at war with all the rest. In this citizenship of the universe consists man's true freedom, and his liberation from the thralldom of narrow hopes and fears. (Russell, 1912, pp. 248–249)

A Recovery Resilience Practice may, quoting Russell, enlarge "not only the objects of our thoughts but also the objects of our actions and our affections" (expanded mode of Natural Functioning) and "with the absence of insistence" (Defusing Requirements) liberate us from our "narrow hopes and fears" (contracted mode of I-System Functioning and addicted mode).

Putting It All Together

We reiterate that the Recovery Resilience Program outlined in this workbook is not in any way designed to replace your existing recovery practices or be a self-standing approach to treating your addiction. A Recovery Resilience Practice is not designed to address all aspects of developing a sustainable recovery lifestyle. It primarily focuses on strengthening your inner resources and helping you take full advantage of your recovery capital. We believe that it is imperative that apart from strengthening your inner resources you also need external support and structure, such as being part of a support group like Twelve-Step fellowships or SMART Recovery or therapy support groups that consistently reinforce your intentions and various recovery skills and practices. In short, a Recovery Resilience Practice is an adjunct to your overall recovery process, whether that is facilitated primarily through self-help groups or psycho-educational support groups.

There are two aspects to having a Recovery Resilience Practice:

(1) The application of a Recovery Resilience Practice in **activities of daily living** as the need arises in the moment, for example, dealing with high-risk situations, triggers, or stressful situations. The seven components of your Recovery Resilience Practice are:

1. Mapping
2. Recognize I-System Activity
3. Sensory Awareness
4. Recognize and Defuse Requirements
5. Defuse Depressor Storylines
6. Defuse Fixer Storylines
7. Experience the Shift

(2) The incorporation of your Recovery Resilience Practice as part of your **daily recovery-oriented routine**. This aspect provides structure to your practice. This is especially important in the early stages of developing a Recovery Resilience Practice.

As with any newly acquired practice, it takes repetition to achieve mastery. There is much evidence that supports the value of having a daily routine as part of a recovery process. You may already have a daily recovery routine as this is a common part of most recovery processes, and if you do we suggest that you incorporate your Recovery Resilience Practice into this daily routine.

We suggest the following routine (if you are working a Twelve-Step program add this to your existing routine):

Morning Routine:
o Do a Map as part of your morning routine
o Incorporate your Recovery Resilience Practice as part of Step Eleven

Evening Routine:
o Incorporate your Recovery Resilience Practice as part of Step Eleven
o Keep a Recovery Resilience Practice Journal where you write down your experience of the day through the lens of a Recovery Resilience Practice. At times it helps to do a Map about the day before writing in your journal. (Note moments of I-System activity – Requirements, Depressor and Fixer Storylines, and addicted mode, moments when you experienced the Shift.) Include this if you are already doing a daily journal as part of your Step Ten practice.

Weekly Routine:
o One day a week, preferably at the end of the week, complete the scales that are included in this workbook. These are especially helpful in the early stages of your practice. And once you are comfortable with your Recovery Resilience Practice, they can fall away, and you can just continue with your daily journaling – something we suggest that you keep on doing regardless of your clean time.

Progress Not Perfection

Now that we have presented all features of a Recovery Resilience Practice, we want to highlight that one of the perils of any personal development process is that we can have Requirements about the outcome of such a process. Requirements can lead to us to continuously measure ourselves against unattainable and perfectionist ideals. Instead of improving our well-being, this adds to our distress and feelings of inadequacy.

Individuals working an addiction recovery program run the risk of succumbing to this common problem. As we have discussed, addicts are often known to have perfectionistic tendencies with overdeveloped inner critics, fueled by low self-esteem and internalized shame. Their shame often drives them relentlessly to prove to themselves and others that they are good enough – keeping them stuck in Sisyphean struggle.

Most recovery programs focus primarily on the "doing" or "what" of recovery, the tangible practice components of a recovery lifestyle. We have referred to these skills and tools as recovery capital. Certainly, this is a crucial component of any sustainable recovery process. But as we have shown in this workbook, another equally important component of recovery is "being" (as opposed to only "doing"), or in other words, paying close attention to "who" is doing these recovery practices – you in an I-System Functioning or addicted mode or you in Natural Functioning mode. In short, each recovery practice can be understood as having two qualities: the *"doing"* or "what" of the practice, and the *"being"* or "who" of the practice. A recovery lifestyle may in fact consist of ostensibly healthy practices, but if these practices are Fixer-driven, they may seriously compromise or even have a long-term destructive effect on your well-being. For example, you could be going to the gym five times a week, but if this is influenced by the Storylines of your Depressor and Fixer (e.g., perfectionism and over-criticalness), it could result in negative outcomes such as over-training and burnout. Another example is participating in a Twelve-Step meeting with an attitude of arrogance and closed-mindedness or with an open attitude of humility, gratitude, and willingness. The attitude of your participation – "who" is at the helm – will profoundly affect the value you get from the practice. It is important that you maintain a healthy balance between *"doing"* and *"being,"* (i.e., the *what* and the *who*). Your recovery program ought not to become another Fixer-driven and ultimately futile attempt (like your addictive behavior) to *"fix what ain't broke."*

For recovery to be sustainable you must work hard – not to fix yourself – but to realize that essentially you are *good enough*. A Recovery Resilience Practice is not about fixing yourself, but rather the slow process of realizing that there is indeed *nothing to fix*.

In Conclusion

Now that we have come to the end of the workbook, we would like to reiterate the Charlie Parker quote mentioned in the Introduction: "If you don't live it, it won't come out of your horn" – which is to say that your Recovery Resilience Practice and your recovery will be sustainable only if you "live it," that is, through ongoing daily practice. With an ongoing Recovery Resilience Practice you will become more intimately familiar with the workings of your I-System. Armed with this awareness, you can simply use your I-System as a compass to warn you that you are drifting off your recovery pathway and use your Recovery Resilience Practice to get back on track.

As we have stressed throughout the workbook, the aim of your Recovery Resilience Practice is to deal with situations and to live your life in Natural Functioning. In this state, you are innately resilient and have more access to your recovery capital – and with continued practice, this leads to flourishing and enhances your capacity to achieve your recovery and life goals.

In conclusion, and reiterating the central premise of the Recovery Resilience Program, recovery is not just about abstaining from alcohol and other drugs, but also about gaining "liberation from the [I-System's] thralldom of narrow hopes and fears" (Russell, 1912, p. 249), and discovering a life and way of being that is joyful and meaningful, and has true freedom.

SUMMARY OF CHAPTER 6

Recovery Resilience Practice

- Do **Mapping** related to any high-risk situation, trigger, or troubling experience.
- **Recognize I-System Activity** by being aware of body tension and mental clutter.
- **Practice Sensory Awareness**.
- **Recognize & Defuse Requirements** when performing daily activities.
- **Defuse Depressor Storylines.**
- **Defuse Fixer Storylines**.
- Recognize your **Depressor-Fixer Cycle** in activities of daily living.
- **Experience the Shift.**
- Complete your Recovery Resilience Journal daily.

On the next few pages please fill out the following:

Addicted Mode Warning Signs: Use the template and write down in the space provided your Addicted Mode Warning Signs for the past week. Try and be as comprehensive as possible.

Flourishing Scale: Complete the scale and calculate and your score, from 1 to 7, for each question over the past week or two.

Recovery Resilience Practice Scale: Complete the scale and calculate and write down the frequency of your Recovery Resilience Skills practice. Indicate whether it was never, hardly ever, occasionally, or regularly.

Addicted Mode Warning Signs

Date: _____

Over the past week write down how your I-System has been active in each of your life dimensions.

	Addicted Mode Warning Signs
Self	
Others	
The world	

Flourishing Scale

Date: _____

Below are eight statements with which you may agree or disagree. Using the 1–7 scale below, indicate your agreement with each item by indicating that response for each statement.

- 7 – Strongly agree
- 6 – Agree
- 5 – Slightly agree
- 4 – Neither agree nor disagree
- 3 – Slightly disagree
- 2 – Disagree
- 1 – Strongly disagree

Indicate your agreement with each item	(1–7)
I lead a purposeful and meaningful life	
My social relationships are supportive and rewarding	
I am engaged and interested in my daily activities	
I actively contribute to the happiness and well-being of others	
I am competent and capable in the activities that are important to me	
I am a good person and live a good life	
I am optimistic about my future	
People respect me	
Total score:	_____

The *Flourishing Scale* was developed by Diener, E., Wirtz, D., Tov, W., et al. (2010). New measures of well-being: Flourishing and positive and negative feelings. *Social Indicators Research*, 39, 247–266.

Recovery Resilience Practice Scale

Date: _____

Over the past week indicate the frequency of each component of your Recovery Resilience Practice. Check the description that most closely reflects your practice: never, hardly ever, or occasionally.

Frequency of Recovery Resilience Practice	Never	Hardly Ever	Occasionally	Regularly
Recognize I-System Activity				
Mapping				
Sensory Awareness				
Recognize Requirements				
Defuse Depressor Storylines				
Defuse Fixer Storylines				
Defuse Requirements				
Experience the Shift				

References

Aarts, H., & Dijksterhuis, A. (2000). Habits as knowledge structures: Automaticity in goal-directed behavior. *Journal of Personality and Social Psychology, 78*, 53–63.

Ahmed. S. H., & Pickards, H. (Eds.) (2019). *The Routledge Handbook of the Philosophy and Science of Addiction*. Routledge.

American Psychiatric Association. (2013). *Diagnostic and Statistical Manual of Mental Disorders*. (5th ed.) American Psychiatric Association.

Arp, R., Smith, B., & Spear, A. (2015). *Building Ontologies with Basic Formal Ontology*. MIT Press.

Badenoch, B. (2017). *The Heart of Trauma: Healing the Embodied Brain in the Context of Relationships*. Norton.

Baer, R. A. (2003). Mindfulness training as a clinical intervention: A conceptual and empirical review. *Clinical Psychology: Science and Practice, 10*, 125–143.

Barber, J. G., & Crisp, B. R. (1995). Social support and prevention of relapse following treatment for alcohol abuse. *Research on Social Work Practice, 5*(3), 283–296.

Baumeister, R. F. (2001). Ego depletion and self-control failure: An energy model of the self's executive function. *Self and Identity, 1*, 129–136.

Bell, S., Carter, A., Mathews, R., et al. (2014). Views of addiction neuroscientists and clinicians on the clinical impact of a "Brain Disease Model of Addiction." *Neuroethics, 7*, 19–27. http://doi:10.1007/s12152-013-9177-9.

Block, S. H., & Block, C. B. (2007). *Come to Your Senses: Demystifying the Mind-Body Connection*. 2nd ed. Atria Books/Beyond Words Publishing.

Block, S. H., Block, C., & Du Plessis, G. (2016). *Mind-Body Workbook for Addiction: Effective Tools for Relapse Prevention and Recovery*. New Harbinger.

Block, S. H, Block, C. B., Tollefson, D., & Du Plessis, G. (2020). *Social Unrest: Resolving the Dichotomies of You/Me and Us/Them*. Utah State University.

Block, S. H., & Du Plessis, G. (2018). *The Mind-Body Bridging Substance Abuse Program Training Manual*. I-Systems Inc. [unpublished training manual].

Blume, A. W., Anderson, B. K., Fader, J. S., & Marlatt, G. A. (2001). Harm reduction Relapse Prevention among Diverse Populations: Progress rather than perfection. In R. H. Coombs (Ed.), *Addiction Recovery Tools: A Practical Handbook*. Sage, 367–382.

Blume, A. W. (2004). Understanding and diagnosing substance use disorder. In R. H. Coombs (Ed.), *Handbook of Addictive Disorders: A Practical Guide to Diagnosis and Treatment*. John Wiley & Sons, 63–93.

Boss, M. (1983). *The Existential Foundations of Medicine and Psychology*. Jason Aronson.

Bowen, S., Chawla, N., & Marlatt, G. A. (2011). *Mindfulness-Based Relapse Prevention for Addictive Behaviors: A Clinician's Guide*. Guilford Press.

Bradshaw, J. (2005). *Healing the Shame that Binds You*. Health Communications Inc.

Brandon, T. H., Tiffany, S. T., Obremski, K. M., & Baker, T. B. (1990). Post cessation cigarette use: The process of relapse. *Addictive Behaviors, 15*, 105–114.

Bransford, J. D., Brown, A. L., & Cocking, R. R. (Eds.). (2000). *How People Learn: Brain, Mind, Experience, and School*. National Academy Press.

Brewer, D. D., Catalano, R. F., Haggerty, K., Gainey, R. R., & Fleming, C. B. (1998). A meta-analysis of predictors of continued drug use during and after treatment for opiate addiction. *Addiction, 93*, 73–92.

Brewer, J. (2017). *The Craving Mind: From Cigarettes to Smartphones to Love – Why We Get Hooked and How We Can Break Bad Habits*. Yale University Press.

Brown, S. A., Goldman, M. S., & Christiansen, B. A. (1985). Do alcohol expectancies mediate drinking patterns of adults? *Journal of Consulting and Clinical Psychology, 53*, 512–519.

Brown, S. A., Vik, P. W., & Craemer, V. A. (1989). Characteristics of relapse following adolescent substance abuse treatment. *Addictive Behaviors, 14*, 291–300.

Butler, D. C. (2003). *Western Mysticism: Augustine, Gregory and Bernard on Contemplation and the Contemplative Life*. Dover.

Cappell, H., & Greeley, J. (1987). Alcohol and tension reduction: An update on research and theory. In H. T. Blane & K. E. Leonard (Eds.), *Psychological Theories of Drinking and Alcoholism*. Guilford Press, 15–54.

Carnes, P. (2008). *Recovery Start Kit. The First 130 Days (Bundle)*. Gentle Path Press.

Cloud, W., & Granfield, R. (2004). A life course perspective on exiting addiction: The relevance of recovery capital in treatment. *NAD Publication* (Nordic Council for Alcohol and Drug Research) *44*, 185–202.

Coles, E., & Viswanath, K. "Health and happiness in policy and practice across the globe: The role of science and evidence." Background paper prepared for the Lee Kum Sheung Center for Health and Happiness, Harvard T. H. Chan School of Public Health, April 2019.

Connors, G. J., Tarbox, A. R., & Faillace, L. A. (1993). Changes in alcohol expectancies and drinking behavior among treated problem drinkers. *Journal of Studies on Alcohol, 54*, 676–683.

Cox, W. M., & Klinger, E. (1988). A motivational model of alcohol use. *Journal of Abnormal Psychology, 97*, 165–180.

Creswell, J. D., Way, B. M., Eisenberger, N. I., & Lieberman, M. D. (2007). Neural correlates of dispositional mindfulness during affect labeling. *Psychosomatic Medicine, 69*(6), 560–565. https://doi.org/10.1097/PSY.0b013e3180f6171f.

Cummings, C., Gordon, J. R., & Marlatt, G. A. (1980). Relapse: Strategies of prevention and prediction. In W. R. Miller (Ed.), *The Addictive Behaviors*. Pergamon Press, 291–321.

Curry, S., Marlatt, G. A., & Gordon, J. R. (1987). Abstinence violation effect: Validation of an attributional construct with smoking cessation. *Journal of Consulting and Clinical Psychology, 55*, 145–149.

Danielian, J., & Gianotti, P. (2012). *Listening with Purpose: Entry Points into Shame and Narcissistic Vulnerability*. Jason Aronson.

Danielian, J., & Gianotti, P. (2017). *Uncovering the Resilient Core: A Workbook on the Treatment of Narcissistic Defenses, Shame, and Emerging Authenticity*. Routledge.

De Beauvoir, S. (1948). *The Ethics of Ambiguity*, trans. B. Frechtman. Philosophical Library.

Du Plessis, G. (2014). An integral ontology of addiction: A multiple object existing as a continuum of ontological complexity. *Journal of Integral Theory and Practice, 9*(1), 38–54.

Du Plessis, G. (2018). *An Integral Foundation for Addiction Treatment: Beyond the Biopsychosocial Model*. Integral Publishers.

Du Plessis, G. (2019a). "Incompatible knots" in harm reduction: A philosophical analysis. In T. Waetjen (Ed.), *Opioids in South Africa: Towards a Policy of Harm Reduction*. Human Sciences Research Council Press.

Du Plessis, G. (2019b). An existential perspective on addiction treatment: A logic-based therapy case study. *International Journal of Philosophical Practice. 5*(1), 1–32.

Du Plessis, G. (2022). Philosophy as a way of life for addiction recovery: A logic-based therapy case study. *International Journal of Applied Philosophy*, *35*(1), 68–87.

Du Plessis, G. (2023). The integrated metatheoretical model of addiction. In E. Ermagan (Ed.), *Current Trends in Addiction Psychology*. Cambridge Scholars Publishing.

Du Plessis, G., Webb, K., & Tollefson, D. (2021). *Resilient Mind Skills Workbook*. Utah State University.

Diener, E., Wirtz, D., Tov, W., et al. (2010). New measures of well-being: Flourishing and positive and negative feelings. *Social Indicators Research*, 39, 247–266.

Earley, P. C. (1994). Self or group? Cultural effects of training on self-efficacy and performance. *Administrative Science Quarterly*, 39, 89–117.

Feder, A., Nestler, E. J., Westphal, M., & Charney, D. S. (2010). Psychobiological mechanisms of resilience to stress. In J. W. Reich, A. J. Zautra, & J. S. Hall (Eds.), *Handbook of Adult Resilience* (pp. 35–54). Springer.

Flores, P. J. (1997). *Group Psychotherapy with Addicted Populations: An Integration of Twelve-Step and Psychodynamic Theory*. The Haworth Press.

Folkman, S., & Lazarus, R. S. (1988). *The Ways of Coping Questionnaire*. Consulting Psychologists Press.

Foote, J., Wilkens, C., & Kosanke, N. (2014). *Beyond Addiction: A Guide for Families*. Scribner.

Frankl, V. (1953). *Man's Search for Meaning*. Pocket Books.

Frankl, V. (1969). *The Will to Meaning: Foundations and Applications of Logotherapy*. New American Library.

Fredrickson, B. L., & Losada, M. F. (2005). Positive affect and the complex dynamics of human flourishing. *American Psychologist*, *60*, 678–686.

Gire, J. T. (2002). A cross-national study of motives for drinking alcohol. *Substance Use and Misuse*, *37*, 215–223.

Granfield, R., & Cloud, W. (1996). The elephant that no one sees: Natural recovery among middle-class addicts. *Journal of Drug Issues*, *26*(1), 45–61.

Greenfield, S., Hufford, M., Vagge, L., et al. (2000). The relationship of self-efficacy expectancies to relapse among alcohol dependent men and women: A prospective study. *Journal of Studies on Alcohol*, *61*, 345–351.

Greeson, J., Garland, E. L., & Black, D. (2014). Mindfulness: A transtherapeutic approach for transdiagnostic mental Processes. In A. Ie, C. T. Ngnoumen, &

E. J. Langer (Eds.), *The Wiley Blackwell Handbook of Mindfulness*. John Wiley & Sons, Ltd.

Gren, L. H., Jaggi, R., Landward, R., Scott Benson, L., & Frost, C. J. (2017). A community health coach-delivered mental wellness intervention: Using mind-body bridging to reduce health disparities in diverse communities. *Pedagogy in Health Promotion, 3*(3), 167–176.

Groves, P., & Farmer, R. (1994). Buddhism and addictions. *Addictions Research, 2*, 183–194.

Hadot, P. (1995). *Philosophy as a Way of Life: Spiritual Exercises from Socrates to Foucault*, trans. Michael Chase. Blackwell.

Hayes, S. C. (2003). Buddhism and acceptance and commitment therapy. *Cognitive and Behavioral Practice, 9*(1), 58–66.

Hayes, S. C., Wilson, K. G., Gifford, E. V., Follette, V. M., & Strosahl, K. (1996). Experiential avoidance and behavioral disorders: A functional dimensional approach to diagnosis and treatment. *Journal of Consulting and Clinical Psychology, 64*, 1152–1168.

Hill, K. (2008). A strengths-based framework for social policy: Barriers and possibilities. *Journal of Policy Practice, 7*(2–3), 106–121. https://doi:10.1080/15588740801937920.

Ho, S. S., & Nakamura, Y. (2017). Healing dysfunctional identity: Bridging mind-body intervention to brain systems. *Journal of Behavioral and Brain Science, 7*, 137–164.

Horney, K. (1950). *Neurosis and Human Growth*. Norton.

Hursthouse, R. (2001). *On Virtue Ethics*. Oxford University Press.

Johnson, R. (1989). *Inner Work: Using Dreams and Active Imagination for Personal Growth*. Harper & Row.

Irvin, J. E., Bowers, C. A., Dunn, M. E., & Wang, M. C. (1999). Efficacy of relapse prevention: A meta-analytic review. *Journal of Consulting and Clinical Psychology, 67*, 563–570.

Jones, B. T., Corbin, W., & Fromme, K. (2001). A review of expectancy theory and alcohol consumption. *Addiction, 96*, 57–72.

Jones, B. T., & McMahon, J. (1996). A comparison of positive and negative alcohol expectancy value and their multiplicative composite as predictors of post-treatment abstinence survivorship. *Addiction, 91*, 89–99.

Kashdan, T. B., & Rottenberg, J. (2010). Psychological flexibility as a fundamental aspect of health. *Clinical Psychology Review, 30*(11), 865–878.

Kabat-Zinn, J. (1994). *Wherever You Go, There You Are: Mindfulness Meditation in Everyday Life*. Hyperion.

Kenny, A. 1978. *The Aristotelian Ethics: A Study of the Relationship Between the Eudemian and the Nicomachean Ethics of Aristotle*. Clarendon Press.

Khantzian E. J. (1997). The self-medication hypothesis of substance use disorders: A reconsideration and recent applications. *Harvard Review of Psychiatry, 4*(5), 231–244. https://doi.org/10.3109/10673229709030550.

Khantzian, E. J., Halliday, K. S., & McAuliffe, W. E. (1990). *Addiction and the Vulnerable Self: Modified Dynamic Group Therapy for Substance Abusers*. Guilford Press.

Khantzian, E. J. (1999). *Treating Addiction as a Human Process*. Jason Aronson.

Kaufman, W. (Ed.). (1997). *Marcus Aurelius Meditations*. Dover Publications

Kohut, H. (1971). *The Analysis of the Self: A Systematic Approach to the Psychoanalytic Treatment of Narcissistic Personality Disorders*. International University Press.

Kohut, H. (1977). *The Restoration of Self*. International University Press.

Kurtz, E., & Ketcham, K. (2002). *The Spirituality of Imperfection: Storytelling and the Search for Meaning*. Bantam Books.

Kramer, R. (1995). The birth of client-centered therapy: Carl Rogers, Otto Rank, and "The Beyond." *Journal of Humanistic Psychology*, 35, 54–110.

Laws, D. R. (1995). Central elements in relapse prevention procedures with sex offenders. *Psychology, Crime and Law, 2*(1), 41–53.

Lazarus, R. S. (1966). *Psychological Stress and the Coping Process*. McGraw-Hill.

Lazarus, R. S., & Folkman, S. (1984). *Stress, Appraisal, and Coping*. Springer.

Levin, J. D. (1995). Psychodynamic treatment of alcohol abuse. In J. P. Barber & P. Crits-Christoph (Eds.),*Dynamic Therapies for Psychiatric Disorders (Axis 1)*. Basic Books.

Lipschitz, D. L., Kuhn, R., Kinney, A. Y., Donaldson, G. W., & Nakamura, Y. (2013). Reduction in salivary α-amylase levels following a mind-body intervention in cancer survivors: An exploratory study. *Psychoneuroendocrinology, 38*(9), 1521–1531.

Lipschitz, D. L., Kuhn, R., Kinney, A. Y., et al. (2015). An exploratory study of the effects of mind-body interventions targeting sleep on salivary oxytocin levels in cancer survivors. *Integrated Cancer Therapies, 14*(4), 366–380.

Lipschitz, D. L., Landward, R., & Nakamura, Y. (2014). An exploratory study of an online mind-body program for poor sleepers in a community sample. *European Journal of Integrative Medicine, 6*(1), 48–55.

Lipschitz, D. L., Olin, J. A., & Nakamura, Y. (2016). A randomized controlled pilot study of a mind-body intervention compared with treatment as usual in the management of insomnia among active-duty military personnel. *European Journal of Integrative Medicine, 8*(5), 769–780.

Litt, M. D., Kadden, R. M., Cooney, N. L., & Kabela, E. (2003). Coping skills and treatment outcomes in cognitive-behavioral and interactional group therapy for alcoholism. *Journal of Consulting and Clinical Psychology, 71*(1), 118–128.

Max-Neef, M. A. (with Antonio, E., & Hopenhayn, M.). (1991). *Human Scale Development: Conception, Application and Further Reflections.* Apex.

McMahon, R. C. (2001). Personality, stress, and social support in cocaine relapse prediction. *Journal of Substance Abuse Treatment, 21*, 77–87.

McPeak, J. D., Kennedy, B. P., & Gordon, S. M. (1991). Altered states of consciousness therapy: A missing component in alcohol and drug rehabilitation treatment. *Journal of Substance Abuse Treatment, 8*, 75–82.

Marlatt, G. A., & Gordon, J. R. (1980). Determinants of relapse: Implications for the maintenance of behavior change. In P. O. Davidson & S. M. Davidson (Eds.), *Behavior Medicine: Changing Health Lifestyles* (pp. 410–452). Brunner/Mazel.

Marlatt, G. A. (1985a). Relapse prevention: Theoretical rationale and overview of the model. In G. A. Marlatt & J. R. Gordon (Eds.), *Relapse Prevention* (1st ed., pp. 280–250). Guilford Press.

Marlatt, G. A. (1985b). Lifestyle modification. In G. A. Marlatt & J. R. Gordon (Eds.), *Relapse Prevention: Maintenance Strategies in the Treatment of Addictive Behaviors* (1st ed., pp. 280–348). Guilford Press.

Marlatt, G. A. (1988). Research on behavioral strategies for the prevention of alcohol problems. *Contemporary Drug Problems, 15*, 31–45.

Marlatt, G. A., & Gordon, J. R. (Eds.). (1985). *Relapse Prevention: Maintenance Strategies in the Treatment of Addictive Behaviors* (1st ed.). Guilford Press.

Marlatt, G. A., Pagano, R. R., Rose, R. M., & Marques, J. K. (1984). Effects of meditation and relaxation training upon alcohol use in male social drinkers. In D. H. Shapiro & R. N. Walsh (Eds.), *Meditation: Classic and Contemporary Perspectives* (pp. 105–120). Aldine.

Marlatt, G. A., Baer, J. S., & Quigley, L. A. (1995). Self-efficacy and addictive behaviour. In A. Bandura (Ed.), *Self-Efficacy in Changing Societies* (pp. 289–315). Cambridge University Press.

Marlatt, G. A., & Witkiewitz, K. (2002). Harm reduction approaches to alcohol use: Health promotion, prevention, and treatment. *Addictive Behaviors, 901*, 1–20.

Maté, G. (2011). *In the Realm of Hungry Ghosts: Closer Encounters with Addiction.* North Atlantic Books.

Milkman, H. B., & Sunderworth, S. G. (2010). *Craving for Ecstasy and Natural Highs: A Positive Approach to Mood Alteration.* Sage.

Miller, W. R., Westerberg, V. S., Harris, R. J., & Tonigan, J. S. (1996). What predicts relapse? Prospective testing of antecedent models. *Addiction, 91*(Suppl.), 155–171.

Nakamura, Y., Lipschitz, D. L., Donaldson, G. W., et al. (2017). Investigating clinical benefits of a novel sleep-focused mind-body program on Gulf War illness symptoms: A randomized controlled trial. *Psychosomatic Medicine, 79*(6), 706–718.

Nakamura, Y., Lipschitz, D. L., Kanarowski, E., et al. (2015). Investigating impacts of incorporating an adjuvant mind-body intervention method into treatment as usual at a community-based substance abuse treatment facility: A pilot randomized controlled study. *SAGE Open, 5*(1).

Nakamura Y., Lipschitz D. L., Kuhn R., Kinney A. Y., & Donaldson G. W. (2013). Investigating efficacy of two brief mind-body intervention programs for managing sleep disturbance in cancer survivors: A pilot randomized controlled trial. *Journal of Cancer Survivorship, 7,* 165–182.

Nakamura, Y., Lipschitz, D. L., Landward, R., Kuhn, R., & West, G. (2011). Two sessions of sleep-focused mind-body bridging improve self-reported symptoms of sleep and PTSD in veterans: A pilot randomized controlled trial. *Journal of Psychosomatic Research, 70,* 335–345.

Narcotics Anonymous World Services, Inc. (1983). *It Works How and Why: The Twelve Steps and Twelve Traditions.* Narcotics Anonymous World Services, Inc.

Nietzsche, F. (2003). *The Joyful Science: With a Prelude in German Rhymes and an Appendix of Songs,* B. Williams (Ed.). Cambridge University Press.

Peterson, C., & Seligman, M. E. P. (2004). *Character Strengths and Virtues: A Handbook of Classification.* Oxford University Press.

Perls, F. (1969). *In and Out the Garbage Pail.* Real People Press.

Perls, F. (1976). *The Gestalt Approach & Eye Witness to Therapy* (2nd Ed.). Bantam Books.

Polk, T. (2015). *The Addictive Brain.* [DVD]. The Great Courses. https://www.thegreatcourses.com/courses/the-addictive-brain.

Rank, O. (1929). *The Trauma of Birth.* Courier Corporation.

Russell, B. (1912). *The Problems of Philosophy.* Oxford University Press,

Smuts, J. C. (1926). *Holism and Evolution.* Macmillan.

Spinoza, B. (1955). *Works of Spinoza: Vol. II,* R. Elwes (Trans.). Dover.

Taylor, J. (2021). *Change Your Life's Direction: Break Free from Your Past Inertia and Chart a Better Future*. Rowman & Littlefield Publishers.

Teyber, E., McClure, F., & Weathers, R. (2011). Shame and the family: Transmission across generations. In R. Dearing & J. Tangney (Eds.), *Shame in the Therapy Hour*. American Psychological Association Press.

Tollefson, D. R., & Phillips, I. (2015). A mind-body bridging treatment program for domestic violence offenders: Program overview and evaluation results. *Journal of Family Violence, 30*(6), 783–794.

Tollefson, D. R., Webb, K., Shumway, D., Block, H., & Nakamura, Y. (2009). A mind-body approach to domestic violence perpetrator treatment: Program overview and preliminary outcomes. *Journal of Aggression, Maltreatment, and Trauma, 18*(1), 17–45.

Tollefson, D. R. (2018, May). *Applications of mind-body bridging in social work. Presentation given at the International Mind-Body Bridging Conference: Origin, Theory and Practice*. University of Utah in Salt Lake City, Utah, United States.

Ulman, R. B., & Paul, H. (2006). *The Self Psychology of Addiction and Its Treatment: Narcissus in Wonderland*. Routledge.

VanderWeele, T. J. (2017). On the promotion of human flourishing. *Proceedings of the National Academy of Sciences of the United States of America,* 31:8148–8156.

VanderWeele, T. J. (2020). Activities for flourishing: An evidence-based guide. *Journal of Positive Psychology and Wellbeing,* 4:79–91.

Vernon, A., & Doyle, K. A. (2017). *Cognitive Behavior Therapies: A Guidebook for Practitioners*. John Wiley & Sons, Inc.

Weil, A. (1972). *The Natural Mind*. Houghton Mifflin.

Wells, A. (2005). Detached mindfulness in cognitive therapy: A metacognitive analysis and ten techniques. *Journal of Rational-Emotive and Cognitive-Behavior Therapy, 23*, 337–355.

West, R. (2005). *Theory of Addiction*. Blackwell.

West, R. (2017). *100 Key Facts about Addiction*. Silverback Publishing.

West, R., Christmas, S., Hastings, J., & Michie, S. (2019a). Developing general models and theories of addiction. In S. H. Ahmed & H. Pickards (Eds.), *The Routledge Handbook of the Philosophy and Science of Addiction* (pp. 160–172). Routledge.

West, R., Marsden, J., & Hastings J. (2019b). Addiction theories and constructs: A new series. *Addiction, 114*(6), 955-956. https://doi:10.1111/add.14554.

White, W. L. (1996). *Pathways: From the Culture of Addiction to the Culture of Recovery*. Hazelden.

White, W., & Cloud, W. (2008). Recovery capital: A primer for addictions professionals. *Counselor, 9*(5), 22-27.

Wills, T. A., & Shiffman, S. (1985). Coping and substance use: A conceptual framework. In S. Shiffman & T. A. Wills (Eds.), *Coping and Substance Use*. Academic Press.

Winhall, J. (2021). *Treating Trauma and Addiction with the Felt Sense Polyvagal Model*. Routledge.

Wilber, K. (2000). *Integral Psychology: Consciousness, Spirit, Psychology, Therapy*. Shambhala.

Wilson, B. (1976). *Alcoholics Anonymous: The Story of How Many Thousands of Men and Women Have Recovered from Alcoholism*. Alcoholics Anonymous World Services.

Wilson, B. (1987). *Twelve Steps and Twelve Traditions*. Alcoholics Anonymous World Services.

Winkelman, M. (2001). Alternative and traditional medicine approaches for substance abuse programs: A shamanic perspective. *International Journal of Drug Policy, 12*, 337–351.

Xie, H., McHugo G. J., Fox, M. B., & Drake, R. E. (2005). Substance abuse relapse in a ten-year prospective follow-up of clients with mental and substance use disorders. *Psychiatry Serv 56*: 1282–1287.

Yalom, I. D. (1995). *The Theory and Practice of Group Psychotherapy* (4th ed.). Basic Books.

Zoja, L. (1989). *Drugs, Addiction and Initiation: The Modern Search for Ritual*. Sigo.

Notes

Introduction

1. In a recent publication, *Cognitive Behavior Therapies: A Guidebook for Practitioners* (Vernon & Doyle 2017), Mind-Body Bridging (MBB) was compared to therapeutic approaches and other mindfulness-based interventions that are commonly referred to as the third wave of cognitive behavior therapies. Although MBB shares similarities with many of these interventions, there are significant theoretical and methodological differences. The most fundamental difference is that MBB teaches one how to adopt a metacognitive perspective of the mechanisms and affect states (emotional dysregulation) that underly dysfunctional behavior. The I-System Model is based on the premise that a maladaptive metacognitive thinking style, that takes the form of recurrent and inflexible self-referential thinking, recyclical ideation in the form of worry and rumination and attentional fixation on threat, and unhelpful coping and self-regulation strategies, called I-System Functioning, contributes to psychological dysfunction, and the development and maintenance of psychological disorders (Block & Block, 2007; Ho & Nakamura, 2017; Du Plessis, Webb, & Tollefson, 2021). More specifically, the therapeutic focus of MBB is for the individual to develop skills to recognize and manage this metacognitive thinking style, referred to in I-System Model parlance as I-System Functioning, which is seen as a hindrance to the innate resilience of the "true" or "real" self (called Natural Functioning). MBB is based on the premise that in a state of Natural Functioning this innate resilience and capacity for self-actualization spontaneously emerge. Karen Horney (1950) described alienation from the "real self" as the origin of most psychic distress and described the real self as "the 'original' force toward individual growth and fulfilment" (p. 158). According to Horney (1950), this real self is an "intrinsic potentiality" or "central inner force, common to all human beings" (p. 17) that is the core source of development.
2. See Gren, L. H., Jaggi, R., Landward, R., Scott Benson, L., & Frost, C. J. (2017). A community health coach delivered mental wellness intervention: Using mind-body bridging to reduce health disparities in diverse communities.

Pedagogy in Health Promotion, 3(3), 167–176; Lipschitz, D. L., Kuhn, R., Kinney, A. Y., Donaldson, G. W., & Nakamura, Y. (2013). Reduction in salivary α-amylase levels following a mind-body intervention in cancer survivors: An exploratory study. *Psychoneuroendocrinology, 38*(9), 1521–1531; Lipschitz, D. L., Kuhn, R., Kinney, A. Y., et al. (2015). An exploratory study of the effects of mind-body interventions targeting sleep on salivary oxytocin levels in cancer survivors. *Integrated Cancer Therapies, 14*(4), 366–380; Lipschitz, D. L., Landward, R., & Nakamura, Y. (2014). An exploratory study of an online mind-body program for poor sleepers in a community sample. *European Journal of Integrative Medicine, 6*(1), 48–55; Lipschitz, D. L., Olin, J. A., & Nakamura, Y. (2016). A randomized controlled pilot study of a mind-body intervention compared with treatment as usual in the management of insomnia among active-duty military personnel. *European Journal of Integrative Medicine, 8*(5), 769–780; Nakamura, Y., Lipschitz, D. L., Donaldson, G. W., et al. (2017). Investigating clinical benefits of a novel sleep-focused mind-body program on Gulf War illness symptoms: A randomized controlled trial. *Psychosomatic Medicine, 79*(6), 706–718; Nakamura Y., Lipschitz D. L., Kuhn R., Kinney A. Y., & Donaldson G. W. (2013). Investigating efficacy of two brief mind-body intervention programs for managing sleep disturbance in cancer survivors: A pilot randomized controlled trial. *Journal of Cancer Survivorship, 7*, 165–182; Nakamura, Y., Lipschitz, D. L., Landward, R., Kuhn, R., & West, G. (2011). Two sessions of sleep-focused mind-body bridging improve self-reported symptoms of sleep and PTSD in veterans: A pilot randomized controlled trial. *Journal of Psychosomatic Research, 70*, 335–345; Tollefson, D. R., & Phillips, I. (2015). A mind-body bridging treatment program for domestic violence offenders: Program overview and evaluation results. *Journal of Family Violence, 30*(6), 783–794; Tollefson, D. R., Webb, K., Shumway, D., Block, H. S, & Nakamura, Y. (2009). A mind-body approach to domestic violence perpetrator treatment: Program overview and preliminary outcomes. *Journal of Aggression, Maltreatment, and Trauma, 18*(1), 17–45.

3. The Mind-Body Bridging Substance Abuse Program (Block & Du Plessis, 2018) was vetted as an evidence-based intervention by the National Registry of Evidence-Based Programs and Practices (NREPP), a project of the Substance Abuse and Mental Health Services Administration (SAMHSA) of the United States Department of Health and Human Services. This program was rated effective for improving spiritual health; for reducing general substance use; for reducing sleep and wake disorders and symptoms; and for reducing trauma- and stress-related disorders and symptom (See Nakamura et al., 2015).

4. For discussion on flourishing see VanderWeele, T. J. (2017). On the promotion of human flourishing. *Proceedings of the National Academy of Sciences of the United States of America, 114*(31), 8148–8156; and Diener, E., Wirtz, D., Tov, W., et al. (2010). New measures of well-being: Flourishing and positive and negative feelings. *Social Indicators Research, 39,* 247–266. Numerous organizations, international bodies, and governments have taken significant steps toward promoting happiness. However, the movement to promote happiness faces two major obstacles in translating research into policy. The first issue is the lack of clarity surrounding the concept of happiness, particularly how it is defined, measured, and what purpose it serves. Several reports and projects use different terms such as "well-being," "flourishing," and "quality of life," among others, to describe what they are measuring. This diversity of terms highlights the existence of fundamental differences in philosophies and practices, making it challenging to track progress over time and space. In the absence of a consensus on the definition and purpose of happiness, developing, implementing, and evaluating public policies aimed at promoting happiness becomes difficult. See Coles, E., & Viswanath, K. "Health and happiness in policy and practice across the globe: The role of science and evidence." Background paper prepared for the Lee Kum Sheung Center for Health and Happiness, Harvard T.H. Chan School of Public Health, April 2019.

5. The notion of disposition is an important component of Basic Formal Ontology (BFO). See Arp, Smith, & Spear (2015) and West, Marsden, & Hastings (2019b) for a discussion of applying BFO in developing an Addiction Ontology.

6. The Recovery Resilience Program which was developed by the authors at the I-System Institute for Transdisciplinary Studies, Utah State University, builds upon an evidence-based substance use disorder treatment program called the Mind-Body Bridging Substance Abuse Program (see Block & Du Plessis, 2018).

7. A significant component of strengthening personal recovery capital is in developing psychological flexibility. See Kashdan, T. B., & Rottenberg, J. (2010). Psychological flexibility as a fundamental aspect of health. Clinical *Psychology Review, 30*(11), 865–878.

8. See VanderWeele, T. J. (2017). On the promotion of human flourishing. *Proceedings of the National Academy of Sciences of the United States of America, 114*(31), 8148–8156. https://doi.org/10.1073/pnas.1702996114.

9. We understand the good life from a similar perspective to Aristotle's notion of *eudaimonia,* which he thought to be an excellent, flourishing, and happy life. See Kenny A. (1978). *The Aristotelian Ethics: A Study of the Relationship Between the Eudemian and the Nicomachean Ethics of Aristotle.* Clarendon Press.

10. We are currently working on a facilitator's guide for Cambridge University Press that outlines how to facilitate the Recovery Resilience Program in a structured individual or group format.

11. For a discussion on harm reduction approaches see Blume, A. W., Anderson, B. K., Fader, J. S., & Marlatt, G. A. (2001). Harm reduction relapse prevention among diverse populations 59 programs: Progress rather than perfection. In R. H. Coombs (Ed.), *Addiction Recovery Tools: A Practical Handbook.* Sage, 367-382; and Marlatt, G. A., & Witkiewitz, K. (2002). Harm reduction approaches to alcohol use: Health promotion, prevention, and treatment. *Addictive Behaviors,* 901, 1–20.

12. See Du Plessis, G. (2019a). "Incompatible knots" in harm reduction: A philosophical analysis. In T. Waetjen (Ed.), *Opioids in South Africa: Towards a Policy of Harm Reduction.* Human Sciences Research Council Press, for a discussion of conceptual challenges in harm reduction approaches.

13. See Diener, E., Wirtz, D., Tov, W., et al. (2010). New measures of well-being: Flourishing and positive and negative feelings. *Social Indicators Research, 39,* 247–266.

1 Dealing Effectively with High-Risk Situations

1. See Wills, T. A., & Shiffman, S. (1985). Coping and substance use: A conceptual framework. In S. Shiffman & T. A. Wills (Eds.), *Coping and Substance Use.* Academic Press.

2. See Kenny, A. (1978). *The Aristotelian Ethics: A Study of the Relationship Between the Eudemian and the Nicomachean Ethics of Aristotle.* Clarendon Press.

3. See Marlatt, G. A., & Gordon, J. R. (1980). Determinants of relapse: Implications for the maintenance of behavior change. In P. O. Davidson & S. M. Davidson (Eds.), *Behavioral Medicine: Changing Health Lifestyles* (pp. 410–445). Brunner/Mazel.

4. See Baer, R. A. (2003). Mindfulness training as a clinical intervention: A conceptual and empirical review. *Clinical Psychology: Science and Practice,* 10, 125–143.

5. The practice of Sensory Awareness shares similarities with metacognitive therapy, see Normann, N., & Morina, N. (2018). The efficacy of metacognitive therapy: A systematic review and meta-Analysis. *Frontiers in Psychology, 9,* 2211. https://doi.org/10.3389/fpsyg.2018.02211

6. See Kramer, Robert (1995). The birth of client-centered therapy: Carl Rogers, Otto Rank, and "The Beyond." *Journal of Humanistic Psychology, 35,* pp. 54–110.

2 Coping with Cravings and Triggers

1. Bell, S., Carter, A., Mathews, R., et al. (2014). Views of addiction neuroscientists and clinicians on the clinical impact of a "Brain Disease Model of Addiction." *Neuroethics 7,* 19–27. https://doi:10.1007/s12152-013-9177-9.
2. Adapted from the six recovery dimensions in Du Plessis (2018), *An Integral Foundation for Addiction Treatment: Beyond the Biopsychosocial Model,* which was informed Ken Wilber's (2000) integral metatheory.
3. The suggestion of the Twelve-Step program and the Recovery Resilience Program as recovery being a way of life guided by virtues (called spiritual principles in Twelve-Step philosophy) is congruent with the notion of "philosophy as a way of life." It (see Du Plessis, 2022, "Philosophy as a way of life for addiction recovery") has been suggested that "philosophy as a way of life" is a compelling and legitimate recovery pathway for individuals in addiction recovery, as one of many pathways to recovery. Philosophy as a way of life, inspired by the work of the French scholar Pierre Hadot (1995), is based largely on the practice of "spiritual exercises," intended to transform the practitioner's way of perceiving the world, and hence their mode of being, to enable them to lead a freer, more happy existence.

4 Break the Addiction Cycle

1. With its foundation in social work, the strengths-based approach focuses on an individual's self-determination and strength. See Hill, K. (2008). A strengths-based framework for social policy: Barriers and possibilities. *Journal of Policy Practice, 7*(2–3), 106–121. https://doi:10.1080/15588740801937920.

6 Your Recovery Resilience Practice

1. See Hursthouse, R. (2001). *On Virtue Ethics.* Oxford University Press.
2. See Butler, D. C., (2003). *Western Mysticism: Augustine, Gregory and Bernard on Contemplation and the Contemplative Life.* Dover.

Index